12 Months
of Marketing
for Salon and Spa

From Single Chair to Multi-Station to Chain

Ideas, Events and Promotions for Salon and Spa
Stylists • Estheticians • Therapists • Managers • Owners

Elizabeth Kraus

Owner/CEO, Be InPulse Branding Marketing & Design

12monthsofmarketing.net

Branded and customized Distributor and Manufacturer
"12 Months of Marketing for Salon and Spa" calendar versions available.

12 Months of Marketing for Salon and Spa

by Elizabeth Kraus

Owner/CEO, Be InPulse Branding Marketing & Design

12monthsofmarketing.net

Branded | Customized Distributor or Manufacturer "12 Months of Marketing for Salon and Spa" or Branding calendars, seminars and other resources available.

Author/Editor: Elizabeth Kraus
Cover and Interior Design/Layout: Elizabeth Kraus (Be InPulse Branding, Marketing & Design)

Printing History: 2010 First Edition

ISBN :9781451515954

To my parents, Jim and Sheryll—
who always made me believe that everything is possible.

To my children,
Amanda, Eric, Sarah, Sam, Noa and Rania—
whose possibilities are endless.

To my husband, Dan—
who brought my heart back to life, makes me laugh
and makes sure I believe in myself.

contents

12 Months of Marketing for Salon and Spa

page	section	description
6	0	forward
12	1	marketing essentials
		pg 12 basic collateral and use
		pg 24 space
		pg 26 cooperative and cross marketing
		pg 32 communications and event checklist
		pg 39 social media marketing and 'buy local' campaigns
42	2	january "bubble bath marketing"
		pg 50 event and promotion ideas
		pg 57 planning, calendar and worksheets
62	3	february "pet peeve marketing"
		pg 67 event and promotion ideas
		pg 73 planning, calendar and worksheets
78	4	march "marketing for the single shingle"
		pg 82 event and promotion ideas
		pg 89 planning, calendar and worksheets
94	5	april "where the clients are"
		pg 98 event and promotion ideas
		pg 105 planning, calendar and worksheets
110	6	may "accidental marketing"
		pg 113 event and promotion ideas
		pg 118 planning, calendar and worksheets

page	section	description

122	7	june "get the bounce back"
		pg 125 event and promotion ideas
		pg 131 planning, calendar and worksheets

136	8	july "add-on marketing"
		pg 140 event and promotion ideas
		pg 146 planning, calendar and worksheets

150	9	august "diversion-proof marketing"
		pg 153 event and promotion ideas
		pg 159 planning, calendar and worksheets

164	10	september "visibility in a sea of sameness"
		pg 167 event and promotion ideas
		pg 172 planning, calendar and worksheets

176	11	october "loosen up tippers (in any economy)"
		pg 180 event and promotion ideas
		pg 186 planning, calendar and worksheets

190	12	november "remodel marketing"
		pg 193 event and promotion ideas
		pg 198 planning, calendar and worksheets

202	13	december "out with the old, in with the new scene stealers"
		pg 206 event and promotion ideas
		pg 211 planning, calendar and worksheets

| 216 | | acknowledgements and resources |
| | | pg. 217 observances cited, acknowledgments |

5

forward

For salon and spa industry professionals from Single Chair/Independent Salon Owners to Multi-Station to Chain—

Ideas, Events and Promotions for Salon and Spa Stylists • Estheticians • Therapists • Managers • Owners

12 Months
of Marketing
For Salon and Spa

where the clients are

This has happened to all of us; you were in a conversation with a client, co-worker or friend who presented you with a problem or even asked outright for you to help them think of a solution. However, once you began to offer suggestions they switched quickly into "nope, can't do that" and "that won't work" absolute negativity mode, and within a few minutes you shut down the creativity feeling almost bruised by the way your suggestions or ideas were eliminated like so many ducks shot in a pond. You left the encounter with a strong suspicion that they would rather wallow in their misery than actually try to do something to solve the problem.

What about you? Are you wallowing? Are you in a place where you can identify the things that are holding you back professionally or the areas where your business needs to grow? Is the prospect of doing something new, taking risks and changing the way you have "always" done things something that scares the bejeepers out of you, or do you welcome the turbulence of change because of the corresponding opportunities for adventure, variety and trying new things?

Some salons have seen female clients extend the time between routine hair maintenance services from six to eight or even ten weeks (or more), taking on their own hair color and purchasing care and treatment products formerly purchased in the salon or spa from retail stores. Clients need lower cost hair cutting services and families have to make every dollar count. In the spa and luxury services segment of the industry the disparity between the old normal and the new normal is even greater. Some spa clients have stopped coming altogether; others who used to visit weekly are now just coming once a month or once a quarter.

How much can you allow business to slow before you have to take on a second job or leave the industry altogether? What are you doing to create a new normal of your own that transcends economic factors? What are you doing to take back control of your business, growth of your client base, retail sales and income?

Salon and spas are natural settings for themed event and promotions. You have the ability to tailor packages, products and incentives for nearly every holiday and major life event – from new jobs to new babies to graduations to weddings to anniversaries to 'girlfriend' outings or dates. You see clients at a frequency to easily provide them with ever-changing merchandising displays and seasonal and personal gift suggestions.

When it comes to defining growth and success in the salon and spa, we have over-simplified the answers. Traditional thinking suggests that there are only two ways to be more profitable: Get new clients into the salon (or spa) or increase sales of products and services to existing clients once they are there.

that is limited thinking

There are many ways to build business beyond the simplicity of these two concepts, but you have to learn to think without the old limitations. Yes, you can and should go after new clients and yes, you have to sell products and services to existing clients.

But there are more ways to get clients into the chair than to wait, hoping they will call for an appointment, and there are more opportunities to sell products, services and add-on services than only those times when the client is in the chair. In the same way that the internet's social media web sites have blurred the lines between business and personal, you can evolve your business into a social, tribal site for your clients that blurs the lines between their service appointments and their social, professional and family lives.

Create a bigger, more influential role for your business in the lives of your clients:

» Generate more referrals, increase the frequency of client contacts and entice your clients to join your "tribe."

» Add new (and sometimes non-traditional) services and products to meet more needs of clients.

» Create incentives for loyalty, retail sales, service packages, multiple sales, double bookings and referrals.

» Meet more needs of your clients: social, intellectual, ego, health, wellness, education, personal development, networking – and more.

» Create a haven, an oasis, a creative space, a third space, a social setting, a place to escape or a place to gather.

» Be the facilitator for your clients within the community; link them with other businesses, community leaders, education, with schools and charity resources and great causes in your community.

» Tap deep pools of potential clients.

» Be the voice of change, conscience and progress in your community. Grow your professional and personal ability to lead and influence others and strengthen your reputation in the community.

» Have fun – and be a place where people have fun – listen to great music, laugh, eat, and escape from the doom and gloom of the rest of the media that bombards them!

12 Months of Marketing for the Salon and Spa is a compilation designed to help the salon or spa professional maximize their use of time, energy and marketing dollars while also achieving maximum impact. The salon and spa industry is so unique in composition: represented in some areas by the booth rental market and a high volume of 'single chair' salon owners, by home-based salons, by commission or salary-based multi-chair salons and even by multi-location chains. Business type, size and resources notwithstanding, this publication can be used by any salon or spa professional to help build business, regardless of space or resources available, and regardless of retail products or services offered.

Regardless of the size of your business, the needs shared by salon and spa professionals whether they are part of a salon with one station or many are largely the same:

- » Gaining new clients, increasing referrals, growing prospect lists
- » Retaining clients, increasing loyalty, bringing clients in more often
- » Selling retail products, selling add-on services, increasing average ticket per client
- » Keeping appointment books full and pre-booked and minimizing the time between client visits
- » Improving profitability and growing the business to the desired level to be positioned for the future

build on what you know

This book is not intended to replace the foundation received educationally in order to become a professional within this industry; it is the next level in developing your marketing skills and should build upon it. The tried and true methods for how to build business and increase your own client base by providing purposeful, devoted customer service and continual development of technical skills through continuing professional education still apply. But it is my hope that this book releases your creative side in growing your business, nurtures unity of desire and purpose for building business among your team, and creates a greater position of influence for you in your client's lives so that you become the first place they think of when it comes to purchasing gifts or pampering themselves. I hope that as a result of this book, you are inspired and empowered to create a more vital role in the lives of your clients, both for you as a professional and for your salon or spa as a business.

it will take some work on your part

You cannot create much buzz, loyalty, or growth without thinking outside the box and going outside the walls of your business. Purchasing retail promotions and posting shelf and display pieces are helpful basics but they do not bring new clients in the door, they do not persuade clients to purchase services or products, and they do not engender customer loyalty or referrals. Planning and distributing flyers or sending postcards for an event does not bring in RSVPs or ensure attendance. Creating a rewards program or selling discounted client services does not keep the books full.

Filling the books, engendering client loyalty, creating buzz worthy, well-attended customer events, crafting memorable client experiences and selling through retail promotions and products takes work on your part. Getting outside of your own walls, engaging in more frequent print and e-mail communication, utilizing more channels for marketing in the salon, in the community, through the press and online, making new contacts, networking, creating meaningful business co-marketing opportunities – these are the kind of activities that *12 Months of Marketing for Salon and Spa* is meant to stimulate.

Each month includes themed ideas, worksheets, inspiration and structure to help you create and strengthen your own brand and build your business:

» An overview of the basic business tools you should not be without

» A customer and community-centric approach to marketing

» When it comes to space in-salon or out, and what to do if you don't have a space of your own

» Cooperative, cross and targeted marketing, and how to build effective business partnerships in order to execute a full scale plan with a team or on your own

» Holiday, fun and obscure observances for inspiration in creating events and promotions beyond those suggested in the calendar

» A robust set of ideas to create a cohesive, compelling promotional plan including specific "big idea" themes with details for planning, implementing, promoting, and executing plus bonus event and promotion ideas

» Supporting charitable endeavors while building business

» Specific recommendations for retail and event partners

» A pattern of activities to help you routinely collect a large communications database for print and e-mail

» Planning and tracking worksheets to list and track your salon's specific retail, event and service goals and to track results

» Suggested working calendars for ordering, planning, communicating, and events dates with specific tasks included to keep you on track and keep the schedule manageable

» The 'what, when and how' to communicate to clients, make changes to decor, merchandising and retail promotions - and more

Additional resources are available online at 12monthsofmarketing.net to help you obtain support and other materials you need.

If it seems overwhelming, just start with one main idea per month (or per quarter) and build from there.

Look ahead!

Work through the book at least 2-3 months into the future; or better yet, mix and match from the collection in a way that works for your business to create a truly cohesive 12-month marketing plan. There are enough ideas in this book to be stretched out and incorporated into your marketing plan for years to come. Utilize each month's collections of ideas and brainstorm with staff - or even clients - to create unique promotions and events that most effectively engage your clientele and staff.

Visit www.12monthsofmarketing.net for more.

Marketing Basics:
A Few Things You
Can't Live Without

Business Cards

Simply (but adamantly) put, do not walk out the door without your business cards. Before you open the salon or spa (or stylist station) each day, ensure that you have business cards on hand in a place where clients will see and feel free to take one. Set up a point of purchase display with the overt suggestion that the client take a card to give to a friend, noting any referral rewards or incentives that you offer.

Keep business cards at your fingertips throughout the day (whether you are in or out of the salon or spa). Give one to the cashier who staffs your local wine shop during tastings, to the man or woman who regularly processes your order at the grocery store, the one who makes your non-fat, no whip venti mocha; you come into contact with many people every day who represent their own networks of potential referrals to your salon or spa.

The best way to ask for new clients or referrals is to ask those who (at least on some level) already know and like you. Beyond personal referrals, each of these types of contacts also represents potential clients within their businesses. Would any of the businesses you frequent each day or week be willing to display some of your marketing collateral? Can you create a simple business card exchange with these businesses? (They display your cards in a public area, and you return the favor.)

For the cost per square inch, Business Cards are probably the most effective and cost-efficient piece of collateral in your arsenal. They pack the most critical information into the smallest space possible and still give you the opportunity to display the gist of your brand. A mere 2" x 3.5" rectangle of space, yet with infinite possibilities to express unique style, speak to your strengths, and most importantly, give people both a reason and the means to contact you.

Business cards are a universally recognized piece of marketing collateral that are storable in wallets or organizers, easy to use for ads, easy to give away to others, and are usually kept. Put your referral reward or new client offer right on your card. Make it a goal to give away at least one business card a day – and never give just one, always give two – a second one to give away.

Note Cards

As a tool for expressing appreciation, sending best wishes, sympathy, congratulations and other heartfelt sentiments, a personal note card remains unsurpassed in its ability to convey poignant, genuine thoughts and feelings from the sender to the recipient - and again – for an incredibly low cost in a very small space. Like the business card, it is an item that you can have customized for yourself as a stylist or your salon; to your strengths, your brand, and your creativity.

Despite the number of times it is cited as an effective interpersonal marketing tool in every service or sales industry, the sending of personal note cards is still rarely done. Few and far between are the professionals who make it a regular part of their working regimen; but in most cases, those professionals are more successful than their peers. Not just because they send note cards, but because they recognize the value of a genuine, personal touch when it comes to how they do business. Sending a personal note card to thank or touch base with a client tells them something about who you are, on the inside. It tells them that you are genuinely interested in them; that you value them enough to expend the time and expense needed to demonstrate your appreciation to them.

Make it your goal to thank your clients, 100% of the time. Your clients do not owe you their patronage, no matter how skillfully you cut and style their hair, care for their skin, manicure their nails, apply their cosmetics, or massage their tired limbs. Consumers can choose from a number of salon or spa professionals for any service in any city; and in the current economy, they can afford to be selective in how and where they spend their dollars. Be appreciative! Let your clients know that you appreciate them entrusting you with their hair, skin, nails, etc. Thank them for their business. Thank them for their referrals. Thank them for their loyalty and patronage.

Sending a personal note card is a simple but extra-ordinary act that can help to set you apart and enhance all of your professional relationships. Set yourself apart. Send Thank You notes to clients. Send Thank You notes to individuals who interview you, to those who teach, educate, or mentor you. Send Thank You notes to other stylists who make a difference in your life. Even send thank you notes to vendors, sales consultants, or professional products stores that provide you with good service.

You will be remembered, you will change someone's day for the better. You do not know how much a few kind words may mean to the recipient, and you do not know when this act will open doors for you through the impression that you make on other professionals within the industry.

Reminders

What happens when your dentist sends you a reminder to make an appointment for your six-month checkup? You call and make the appointment! Reminder phone calls, e-mails, text messages (or even actual postcards) can work for you, too, especially if you do not regularly rebook most clients at the time of their appointment.

Send clients a re-booking reminder by e-mail, text, telephone or postcard highlighting special promotions you are offering or events that you have planned. Depending on how quickly your books fill up, send this reminder 2-3 weeks after an appointment for female clients, and 1 week after an appointment for a male client.

Make it is easy for clients to contact you by including the phone number they should call to book the appointment and suggesting appointment times you know remain slow on your books (or times similar to those the client usually selects). If your clients already pre-book, then send a reminder card one week prior to their scheduled appointment.

The reminder might also include the offer of an incentive for booking add-on services such as a color or texture service, manicure, massage or other service at the same time as their hair cutting service. Or let the reminder card pave the way for retail sales by highlighting products you know would be appropriate for the client or products that are new, improved or available at a special price.

Follow up by using the products you suggested or setting out a 'try me' sample at their appointment. Remind them of the benefits of the products and make sure a retail size is available at hand at their point of purchase. If you make discussion of retail products an organic part of each appointment, you will increase retail sales without feeling as though you have had to put 'hard sell' moves on a client.

If you are a stylist and your salon or spa does not provide print materials such as postcards or notecards, there is no reason that you should not take the initiative to ensure your own success and build your own clientele using direct mail reminders. Investments that you make in yourself are never wasted; going the extra mile may be the difference in your career and will always set you apart from those who wait for clients to come to them.

There are many resources for purchasing your own supplies, and many printers who would be happy to help you develop personalized stationery. You might also consider working with other stylists in your salon to purchase personalized materials for each stylist (you may have increased buying power when you purchase supplies in larger quantities).

Thank You Notes

A close relation to the Reminder, the Thank You Note is never out of style and is always appropriate. For those hesitant to use proactive Reminders, the Thank You note can serve the same purpose with a softer touch. If you are worried that thanking every customer will be an overwhelming task or you fear incurring associated expenses (the two objections I most often hear from stylists), then break it down into smaller groups, being sure that your most valued clients receive the highest priority.

Start your day in the right frame of mind. If your regular daily routine means sleeping until the last minute, throwing your hair back, doing your makeup in the rearview mirror, swigging that first coffee in 60 seconds and tackling your first client, use this moment in time to resolve to change the way you start your day.

Give yourself enough time to care for your own skin, hair, and inner self (just as you instruct your clients to do). Arrive at the salon (or your favorite coffee locale) with an extra 20 minutes to spare and take a few moments to write short note cards to thank each client from the day before for choosing you. Or, work ahead and pre-complete a thank you note to give to each client that day following their appointment. Make a suggestion for their next service date, an add-on service you are "dying to try" on them, or a product that could improve their hair, skin, or makeup.

Or plan to end each day in a spirit of gratitude by taking 20 minutes in your favorite "third space" or while lounging at home to write thank you notes to the clients of that day. Take a few minutes to remember what each client shared with you while in the chair, trusting you to make them look and feel better, and send out some positive wishes on their behalf into the universe. It is easy to write thank you notes to your best clients – to those who brought sunshine or laughter into the salon and took retail products away with them.

But thank you notes are not for cowards. You might be able to transform what was a negative experience into a positive one by writing a thank you note to the client who left you feeling deflated because they did not appreciate your work, or who used their appointment as an excuse to vent all their negative emotions – on you. It might be the hardest thank you that you ever wrote, an apology for the dissatisfaction they felt along with a thank you for what they brought to your attention, and a hope that they will give you an opportunity to change their experience. It might not bring an immediate financial return, but it does put you squarely on the high road and may give you both the opportunity to improve personally and to salvage a client for long term business and even referrals. Often a negative experience will not necessarily mean the loss of a client, but how you handle the negative feedback will.

Money is not a significant object because branded note cards can be purchased from commercial printers at a low cost and generic cards can be purchased at your local dollar or discount store. When you consider the cost of investment, 5 minutes of your time, as little as 5, 10, or 20 cents for supplies plus a stamp; what is the return on investment when the client books the repeat visit? What is the return on investment when they add-on services you suggested or come to their next appointment in a frame of mind ready to purchase the products you recommended?

Promotions and Professional Salon Products

As a marketing professional, I have no trouble sharing my passions and convictions when it comes to marketing. Generating ideas to help business to grow, to know and develop a strong brand, or develop a cohesive, effective marketing plan is something I do not only because it is my product, but because it is my passion.

It is time for you to stop being apologetic and hesitant when it comes to telling clients which products and services they should purchase to look and feel better.

You have spent years learning your trade, trying products, gaining knowledge, and developing technical skills. You have years of experience applying your knowledge and skills on a variety of clients, further honing your instincts so that you are uniquely qualified to make unparalleled suggestions to your clients in order to improve their hair health and appearance, to tailor their hair and makeup to their face and body type, to give them a certain "look" that reflects their personal style, and recommend products to improve their skin and hair health and appearance. You have invested thousands of dollars in your own personal product research as well as in obtaining products for use in the salon - so tell them!

Tell clients about products that will improve and enhance their appearance. Tell clients what you personally love about your favorite products. Tell them about the services they should consider above the basic services they usually purchase from you. Tell them about products new to the salon, new technologies in products or techniques and new skills you or your staff have obtained through continuing education. Offer to provide them with mini versions of add-on services to try at their next appointment. Have before-and-after pictures on hand to demonstrate the results of makeovers, hair color, skin treatments, etc.

When it comes to products, many manufacturers' promotions follow a schedule designed to have retail sales stimulated by corresponding back bar product experiences. Use direct mail to tell your clients what they can expect at their next visit, give them the experience at their appointment, tell them about the product again, and make sure the retail size is available for them at the point of purchase. You will be giving them four sales pitches – without ever having to make one.

Referrals

Ask any number of business owners what their best source of new business is and I predict that most – if not all – declare, "word of mouth." If you believe that current clients are your best source of new clients, use e-mail and direct mail communications to suggest and incentivize them to refer their friends, family, and co-workers to your salon. Send clients a postcard each quarter with your new client and referral incentives to pass forward to a friend or family member.

Design a reward both for the existing client (for the referrer) as well as for the new referral (as a new client). If possible, have them book appointments together so that they can share transportation or use the event as an excuse for a girls, guys or couples night out.

Keep it simple. Take a pre-set dollar amount (such as $5, $10, or even $20, depending on the average price of services) off the bill for both the client new to the salon and the client who referred them at their next appointments, or follow up by sending the new client and the referring client a gift card to be used at their next visit (which is another great moment to remind them to book their next appointment, thank them for their patronage, and make suggestions for the future).

A Web site

One of the toughest aspects of running any business that employs people is the "employing people" part. As salon owners you have no choice but to become an instant staff development director, human resource manager, conflict resolution expert and consummate motivator to the best of your abilities.

Even then, people do not always play along. What may work to incentivize some staff does not interest others. Sometimes, no matter how far you go to empathize, sympathize, motivate and interest your employees, they choose not to come along for the ride when it comes to initiatives designed to build your business and increase revenues. Some employees even demonstrate personal lack of concern for your business – coming in late, skipping employee meetings, refusing to participate in sales initiatives, refusing even to help grow their own clientele.

Worse, no matter how hard you try to develop a mutually respectful, positive climate and culture, some employees undermine your efforts – sometimes subtly and sometimes in outright subversion to the goal.

Wonder what this has to do with a web site?

As someone who has been preaching the value of a web site and e-mail as necessary components to any marketing plan for professionals in the salon and spa industry for several years, I have been told by some distributor sales consultants (and even some salon owners) that their clients "do not use the web." I feel your subtle (and sometimes not so subtle) resistance when I tell you that your business does, in fact, need a web site. I still hear individuals within the industry say they are afraid that they will make their customers "mad" if they e-mail them.

Since marketing and business arguments have still not overcome your objections to putting technology to work for you, I want to give you a more self-centered reason to add a web site and e-mail to your marketing arsenal.

The internet and e-mail will work for you too; but unlike some of the people who work for you, but they will not talk back, they will not undermine your efforts to grow business, nor will they create a negative undertone by grumbling or going off message. They will work for you, showing up day in and day out, at any time day or night, 24 hours a day, 365 days a year. They will support your sales initiatives, help generate new business and play an active role in attracting clients new to the area and those looking to make a change from the competition. They will unapologetically deliver your marketing and advertising messages to both clients and prospects without fear of rejection or offending people.

The beauty of putting technology to work for you in the form of e-mail and the internet is that you can create the best version of your business for display. You can tell clients about products that stylists 'forget' to mention. You can promote new stylists, celebrate personal events of staff and clients, you can congratulate and give kudos, and espouse worthy causes. You can tailor communications to your clients desired frequency and interests. You can create leverage needed to attract other businesses for cross marketing or conducting cooperative events and marketing campaigns.

Even now, some salon professionals believe that they do not need a web site and are intimidated by the prospect of building one (or afraid of the cost). If your eyes are glazing over right now, stay with me! A web site does not have to be a bank-buster and it does not have to be complicated. It can be as simple as a one page site costing as little as a couple hundred a year (compare the cost of that with your yellow page listing) that includes contact information, or a multi-page site for your home page plus contact/location, menu, a subscription form for newsletters, promotions and event notifications, and a special web offer for current or new clients. Simply put, you have to have a web site, because your clients use the web.

As of mid-way through the last decade, more than half of all Americans spent more than an hour online every day, and more than half of U.S. adults had high speed internet service in their homes. Those statistics go up every year, and they are even higher for working professional men or women, moms, boomers, and especially for Generation X on down (individuals in your prime demographics).

Your clients and prospective clients will be looking for you – or someone like you – online. An ever-increasing number of people go to the internet first (and exclusively) to find local businesses, rather than the phone book. You will be Googled, Yahoo'ed and otherwise searched for. A web site is your 24 hours x 7 days a week x 365 days per year billboard to the world. You can start with a landing page for as little as a couple hundred dollars a year or build a complete online community.

E-Mail

As powerfully effective as note cards are when it comes to expressing emotion, e-mail is to overall communications. Even if you have never used a computer, you can still use e-mail as a communications tool for your business.

How? Simple. If you really do not want to learn to use e-mail, hire a local high school or college student to conduct your electronic communications. Just a few hours a week will be enough to give you a start on an effective e-mail communications program.

If simplicity is not compelling, price may be. Note cards and postcards are very inexpensive and fairly quick in reaching their destinations, but e-mail is immediate, trackable and FREE. E-mail also has a significantly higher response rate than other forms of direct marketing.

Here are a few ways to put e-mail to work for you:

» Appointment reminders

» Sending directions and contact information

» Thank you notes

» Newsletters

» Promotional service or retail offers for clients

» Event announcements and reminders

» Collecting RSVP's and taking reservations

» Appointment inquiries from your web site

» Cooperative marketing and advertising with your business partners

While not exhaustive, here are a few guidelines for using e-mail:

» Be as personal as possible.

» Keep it brief and readable in a quick sitting.

» Keep e-mail addresses private; when sending a group e-mail, put the e-mail addresses in the "BCC" (blind carbon copy) field, not the "TO" field where they can be seen - and taken - by others.

» Be yourself. Even your e-mail communications reflect the personal brand of you in imagery and language.

» Include inspiration, insight and humor. If something you heard about touched or inspired you, chances are it will inspire and engage others.

» Be protective. If you wouldn't want to read it about yourself, don't write it about someone else. Never, ever share personal information without permission.

» Before you hit 'send' re-read what you have written at least twice; read it out loud to see if it sounds like something that you would say.

» And, if possible, ask a peer to proof-read any communications that you are sending out to groups of clients for language, branding, tone and as your back up to prevent dissemination of any inappropriate information.

100% of the Time

Make it your goal to collect 100% of your client's e-mail addresses, with their permission. Every event, promotion or contest should include basic data collection for clients and prospective clients. Ask for referrals.

Your Menu or Brochure

Another must-have for your business is a menu of services, retail products, or brochure. This piece tells the larger story of the benefits you offer to clients and the style that you bring to the table. A poorly designed menu or brochure with errant or outdated data (or worse - text that is crossed through and written over) actually damages the brand you present to prospective clients, vendors and co-workers. Your job is to help clients present the best version of themselves to the world, and you should think about your marketing collateral, menu, signage and other pieces in the same way. They should all be designed to tell a cohesive story, presenting what is best about your brand, your business and your abilities as a salon or spa professional to the world.

Create (or commission) a menu or brochure designed in harmony with your business card and overall brand that reflects your brand personality and style. Keep it simple so that it can be easily updated, and include it as a printable, downloadable item from your web site. If you offer services where the price varies by stylist or by hair length, put in a range or a starting point (such as "$16 and up) rather than specific price ranges – this gives you the flexibility to charge the correct price for services while still giving the client a general idea of the price. Ask your graphic designer for a low-resolution version appropriate for web download or e-mail attachment in addition to the high-resolution version provided for printing from your office computer or professional commercial printer.

Space

If you have space within your salon or spa to accommodate group events, you are ahead. But if you do not, a lack of physical space to hold events does not have to constrain you. You specialize in using creativity to solve serious problems for your clients, covering problem areas, repairing damage, and fixing mistakes made by others. In some cases you have to think outside of the box in order to find the right 'work around' when traditional treatments cannot be utilized. The same creative spirit you bring to your clients can help you as you acknowledge and overcome things that might otherwise stop you when it comes to marketing and other areas of your business operations, and gaining space for events is a prime example.

You may be able to trade services or products with other businesses that have the space you need for events or include their marketing and advertising materials in your communications to clients and prospects.

Do not shy away from holding events outside of your salon. Partnering with other business can actually put you in the driver's seat because when you bring your clients and prospects in to another location, you are bringing prospects to another business; to a restaurant, wine shop, boutique, hotel or events facility that they may not otherwise have patronized. This gives you leverage to negotiate for space. Approach other businesses knowing that you are doing them a favor by bringing customers to them, and work to negotiate so that the event benefits all participants.

Here are some more ideas for capturing event space:

» In the current economy travel is down significantly; hotels and motels are scrambling to bring in business and should be willing to work creatively with you to utilize corporate meeting, restaurant, banquet, or even vacant rooms to accommodate your group event.

» A local caterer, wine shop or restaurant may have a lobby or meeting area conducive to small group events and would also make an ideal partner for cross marketed offers and cooperative advertising on an on-going basis.

» Most offices and schools (even the smallest corporations) have conference rooms that sit empty for several hours each day and most evenings. If bringing customers to their office does not benefit them, trading stylist's services for the owner or staff may be an option.

» Realtors and insurance agents usually have meeting rooms and can also be a resource for effective targeted cooperative marketing and events. Many of them are also hospitable and skilled at open house and other outreach events and may be able to provide you with valuable ideas. They also value referrals and cross marketing opportunities and (usually) have large lists of contacts.

» Community centers and retirement communities usually have multiple, multi-sized meeting areas and may also be a source of new client prospects on an on-going basis, particularly if you can take some of your services to their facilities for seniors who may have limited transportation ability or physical or medical impediments to travel. This demographic is also highly benefitted by manicure, pedicure and other specialized skin and hair care services.

» A strip mall or retail mall with vacant stores may be willing to rent you space for an event; you are bringing new clients to their retail space, and you have the advantage of showing off your event to mall or street traffic. Take advantage of any passing traffic by posting staff 'outside' to hand out flyers, coupons, special offers, or business cards.

» Local wedding, party and event planners have lists of local venues in all size ranges. Create events that draw crowds of interest to your host facility such as bridal or corporate crowd events.

The point is that a *lack of space* can actually be of benefit to you if you approach the opportunity to obtain space as a way to expand the types of promotions and events you can offer. Seek out business partnerships for cross marketing and cooperative marketing that have what you lack, and who want what you have. Use events and services to create leverage in lowering your costs with space providers and other vendors such as restaurants, caterers, florists, musicians, or wine shops – the possibilities are endless.

Your Marketing

The aforementioned "must-have" items are important components of your overall marketing tool chest. In addition to marketing to current clientele, sending offers, updates, newsletters etc., there are other easy, low cost things you can do to attract new clients:

» Target a business or geographic group of businesses with a special offer. For instance, create a special offer or permanent discount for military families, city employees, teachers, or some other hard-working group. Create simple, copy-able black and white (or color) flyers or postcards which can be placed in their break rooms, lunchrooms, posted on company bulletin boards or even sent out via their electronic newsletters. Provide administrative employees with electronic and paper copies for distribution.

» Participate as a supporter or vendor in your city's summer street fairs, holiday parades, corporate olympics, marathons, and similar events. Find a way to take some of your services 'on the road' in order to demonstrate to passers-by, promote in-salon events, and make appointments. Take some of your most popular or seasonal items for retail sale. Purchase inexpensive salon-branded items for sale or distribution (along with your business card) such as branded nail files, disposable flip-flops, lip balms, mugs, water bottles, bottled waters, pens, etc.

» Tell current clients that you are accepting a limited number of new clients and ask them to refer friends and family to you. Reward current clients for referrals (and thank them).

» Target current clients that have a large circle of acquaintances, co-workers, or other organizational influence with a special referral reward incentive or new client offer.

» Create a significant, special offer for employees of the businesses in your vicinity, especially businesses with which you would like to form marketing and event partnerships.

Cooperative Marketing

For the purposes of *12 Months of Marketing for Salon and Spa*, "cooperative marketing" speaks to marketing activities that you do in cooperation with other salon or spa professionals or with other businesses. It is implied that contacts will be shared to a central source for coordinated marketing or advertising campaigns. You can craft offers that work in conjunction with one another such as a "Get in Shape" package that includes a certain set of your services in combination with the services of a fitness center or instructor, or create separate offers to be offered to the clients of all participating business.

Cross Marketing

Whereas cooperative marketing is working together, cross marketing is crossing over to market to someone else's clients and marketing their services or products to yours. The main benefit to participants is an expanded base of specifically targeted prospective clients; optimally these clients will share many of the traits you would find in your largest demographic target markets. You should still use a central source for marketing so that you do not violate your clients trust by giving their contact information away to another business; or you can simply trade marketing materials for distribution to one another's clients in print or e-mail communications or displays.

Some of the items you might trade for marketing space with other businesses include:

- » business cards or brochures
- » web site links
- » retail space
- » lobby or client waiting areas
- » break room or lunchroom space
- » point of purchase displays

One unintended benefit of Cooperative or Cross Marketing is the implied endorsement of the businesses you partner with. It is also a caution that you expose your clients only to those businesses who will treat them as good as you do!

Marketing Partnerships

Your marketing partnerships will be most effective when you choose partners in context of specific promotions or events, and in relationship to your business, the nature of your clientele and your business goals. For the purposes of _12 Months of Marketing for Salon and Spa_, when the words 'Partnership' or 'Marketing Partners' are used, it refers to an informal partnership (rather than a legal or formal one). While there may be instances where you want to detail responsibilities in writing, most partnerships will be demonstrated in cooperative work together with verbal agreements, trust, and the benefit of the doubt.

Purposefully seek out and establish partnerships with businesses that have something you want (and want something you have) to create leverage and win-win scenarios. Here are some additional considerations to keep in mind when considering businesses you might partner with:

> » Ideal client base – business partners whose ideal or main types of clients share some of the same characteristics or demographics as your ideal clients, such as geographic location, income or home ownership, gender, age, children, disposable income, charitable interests and activities

> » Social basis – partnerships or suggestions from among your current clientele, your family, friends, acquaintances, co-workers or former co-workers, etc.; partnerships whose businesses are represented by some of your current clients

> » Proximity – partnerships with businesses that are located near yours

> » Contact lists – partnerships with independent sellers who already have large client and prospect lists, they are typically familiar with your community and surrounding areas, and they may also have a sizeable sphere of influence in the local community

> » Networking – participate in civic organizations in your community such as your city chamber of commerce, rotary, business roundtable and other social civic organizations

Avoid sharing your contacts with other businesses outright. Whether you have a privacy policy or not, most of your clients believe that they are only giving you their contact information (and permission to communicate with them) and no one else. They will not mind if you endorse other businesses through shared marketing, but they will find it objectionable if you give their information away.

You can honor your clients' trust by agreeing up-front that all businesses participating in cooperative marketing, promotions or events will provide their contacts to a central source or individual. This company or individual will utilize the contacts appropriately for a campaign or marketing activities occurring for an agreed-on period of time, but will not release the contacts to the other businesses involved. This applies both for cooperative and cross marketing campaigns.

Solo Artists, Unite!

On more than one occasion, I have been approached in the mall and complimented on my personal style only to feel completely "shmuck-ified" mere seconds later when the sales pitch from a independent cosmetics seller came on the heels of what I thought was a genuine compliment. The last time that happened, while I still felt the shmuck factor, I did strike up a conversation with this person that was more helpful and it led to an "a-ha" marketing moment: Independent sellers have contact lists, have events know-how, think creatively and are more than open to working partnerships. What's more, their contact lists are likely to include some of your ideal client demographics.

So seek out partnerships for promotions and events with independent sellers - but avoid the shmuck-factor when it comes to your marketing techniques!

Partnerships In Context

Building even just one cooperative or cross marketing partnership can bring new clients to your business and make both businesses more profitable. So building partnerships with several businesses and using them in context with themed promotions, holidays, events and charity fund raisers can make a huge difference in growing your business, growing your client base, engaging and retaining clients, increasing retails sales and building for the future. When created in context, business partnerships can maximize your exposure to your ideal types of prospective clients and give you the means to fill up your events and your books. Partnerships give you the ability to create bigger events and promotions than you could do on your own and reduce your expenses because costs for events and campaigns are shared.

You don't have to partner with everyone.
But partner with someone.

Can't think of where to start? Start with a list of 12. List of set of 12 different kinds of businesses in your community that represent different groups of your target clientele (for instance, a wine shop, a boutique clothier, a candy or chocolatier, a community bank, a dog groomer, an animal charity, a senior center, etc.) Or, simply make a list of the 12 (non-competing) businesses closest in proximity to your location:

- » For each of the 12 businesses on your list, make a list of 3 possible promotions or events you could imagine working on together;
- » write down the names of the next 12 months beginning with the next calendar month beginning about 8 weeks from now;
- » match up the business with which you want to partner with the month when one of the ideas for cooperative promotions or events you thought of would make the most sense; then,
- » approach the owner or manager of that business and suggest the cooperative marketing effort you want to run with them.

Prime Candidates for Partnerships
Shared Contacts • Shared Leads • Shared Costs for Shared Events • Promotions • Packages • Charity Fund Raising

Solo Artists:

Fitness, Jazzercise, and Exercise Instructors, Personal Trainers, Dance and Martial Arts Teachers, Music Teachers Academic Tutors, Handymen, Landscapers, Yard Care, Independent Realtors, Insurance Agents, Animal Trainers, Groomers, Skin Care or Cosmetics Estheticians, Massage Therapists, Wedding, Party and Event Planners, Caterers, Interior Designers Freelance Graphic Designers, Marketing, Advertising and Public Relations Professionals, Independent Sellers, Home-Based Business Owners, Musicians, Bands, Silk Screeners, Promotional Products Vendors, Artists, Woodworkers

Homeowners Services:

Housekeeping Services
Home Repair and Renovation: Flooring, Windows, Roofers, HVAC (Heating and Cooling)
Appliance Repair and Sales
Builders
Community-Based Banks
Financial or Lending Services

Facilities:

Hotels and Motels,
Banquet and Event Facilities,
Restaurants,
Bars and Wine Shops,
Winery Tasting Rooms,
Senior Living and Activity Centers,
Apartment Complexes,
Subdivision and Suburban Community Centers

Retail:

Boutique Clothing, Gift, Art, Stationers and Bookstores, Dry Cleaners, City Merchants (Downtown) or Retail Merchants in closest proximity, Wine Shops, Vitamin or Natural Supplement Stores

Studios and Practices:

Gymnastics, Fitness, and Martial Arts Studios, Sports Practice and Coaching Facilities, Gentlemen's Clubs, Sportsmen's Clubs and Organizations, Smoking Rooms, Music or Dance Studios, Realty Offices, Insurance Offices, Veterinary Services, Kennels, and Grooming Services Dentistry, Cosmetic Dentistry and Orthodontists, Cosmetic Medical and Surgical Services, Specialty or General Medical Practitioners, Chiropractic Services, Naturopathic Services, Manicure-Pedicure, Spray Tan, Massage Therapy and Spa Services

Networking Organizations:

Women-Owned Businesses,
Business-to-Business,
Chamber of Commerce,
Downtown Merchants,

Civic, Social, and Community Organizations:

PTA (Parent-Teacher Association - each school has their own school PTA board and meetings), School District Offices, Private and Public School Offices, Teacher's Unions, Scouting Organizations, Church Groups, MOPS (Mothers of PreSchoolers), City Rotary, Chamber of Commerce or Merchants Associations, Theatres and Theatre Groups, Music and Arts Performance Facilities, Organizations, and Performers, City Hall, Law Enforcement, Emergency Services and City Services Offices, City or County Parks and Recreation Offices and Activities

Community Charitable Service Providers:

Charities usually have large contact lists and run regular campaigns!

Potential Candidates for Partnerships

Communication and Events

Communicate with your clients when they are not in the chair. Every month. And (I cannot stress this enough) make it a part of your regular routine with customers to collect e-mail addresses and verify their contact information. 100% of the time. Every client. Every prospect. Every event.

Despite perceptions you might have personally about spam or junk e-mail, this form of communication can be the best, most effective, and most efficient form of direct marketing in which you engage. It is permission-based; clients expect to be e-mailed and presented with offers. It is free or nearly free and has an exponentially higher return on investment for every dollar spent than other forms of direct marketing. It is personal. It is instant and allows for instant direct response (a recipient can RSVP with a mouse click and a few keystrokes, they don't have to pick up the phone or return something by mail). It is dynamic; clients can be presented with options to 'click' to drive traffic to your web site, to event details, to webstore – anytime, anywhere.

At least once each month, set a planned date to send an e-mail or print newsletter or postcard showcasing your next event, your best current offer, and your most compelling "last chance" promotion.

Client Appreciation Events

If you title an event a "Client Appreciation" event, but you run the event with agenda that makes it obvious that your real goal is to book services, sell packages and push retail, clients will notice. A client-appreciation event should result in each client who attends feeling – well, appreciated!

Plan (all) events from the perspective of the client. It does not mean that you will not book services, do color consultations, sell retail or even packages. It means that the clients who attend will feel as though they were invited to attend because they are important to you. That they have celebrity or VIP status with you. That you do, in fact, have a bead on what they really want and need. That you genuinely want an opportunity to thank them and even to socialize with them.

12 Months of Marketing for Salon and Spa

Include inexpensive salon-branded thank you gifts and put together one or more substantial, client-valued gifts or gift baskets to award at each event in present-to-win drawings. Include some kind of entertainment – music, fashion show, client-awards, humor – something so that it feels like a party, not just business as usual.

Do utilize the event to educate attendees on new products and services in a way that is organic to the nature of the event. Highlight special, new or cutting edge skills and education of staff. Create a path through the salon that allows for free color, cosmetics, or skin consultations. Create "prescription pads" so clients leave with prescribed recommendations for professional products and services for hair or skin.

Sample Event Planning Checklist and Time Lines:

6 - 8 Weeks Before Event

1. Finalize General Event Details:
    » Event date, beginning and end time
    » Goal(s)
    » Venue
    » Theme
    » Menu
    » Entertainment
    » Special promotions on services or retail that will be offered during the event, or for appointments booked at the event.
    » Determine what staff will be needed to work the event

2. Target "Ideal" Attendees: Decide which types of clients (or prospective clients) you would most like to attend, even if you are planning to invite all clients. Knowing who you *most want* to attend will help you shape event details to attract them.

3. Set a Budget: Set a budget, and be realistic. Keep your event as simple as you can, especially if this is your first foray into events. Find businesses to partner with to reduce costs or to enable you to create a larger event than you can afford on your own.

5 Weeks Before Event

1. Assign Responsibilities: Think through how the event will be laid out logistically and what will occur over the course of the event. You cannot do everything yourself. Assign responsibilities among staff, being sure that one or two individuals are assigned to 'float' positions in order to relieve others or fill in.

2. Determine Specifics: Determine what supplies, equipment (tables, chairs, etc.) additional retail, salon-branded items for retail sale or give away, and client-appreciation gifts you will need and purchase (or order) them now to ensure they will be on hand for the event.

3. Work with distributor sales consultants and manufacturers to obtain additional sample items if possible, or buy in sample size items for clients in order to help introduce them to retail products.

4. Purchase at least one salon-branded item which you can either give to clients as a gift item or sell as part of your retail in salon. Salon-branded give away or retail items extend your brand beyond the walls of the salon. How often have you taken a matchbook, a nail file, a button, or another free low-cost item from the stand at a trade show, at a fair, etc.? Small, inexpensive mementos provide a tangible, visible reminder of your business every time they are used or spotted on the shelf.

5. How will you invite people? Create invitations, flyers, postcards, station talkers, bag stuffers and write a script for e-mail invitations, telephone answering machines, or on-hold music.

4 Weeks Before Event

1. Invite People: Post flyers or posters throughout the salon. When it comes to display pieces, less is more. A big, simple, "save the date" with the event date and time that can be seen from several feet away will make more of a visual impact than if you attempt to put every detail and disclaimer onto your signage:

    » at the point of purchase
    » shelf talkers
    » station talkers
    » bag stuffers
    » e-mail communications or your salon newsletter

2. Invite Influential People: Create written invitations to hand deliver to businesses near yours, inviting other business owners and their friends, families and employees to attend. Deliver or mail flyers or invitations to city hall, teachers from local schools, PTAs from local schools, and other women's civic, cultural or business groups. Invite people to attend your events who have influence in social, civic, religious, educational, professional or other circles. Invite the mayor or extend an offer for a free service to a member of city hall, to your local newspaper journalist, to the head of the local PTA, leaders of a local union or trade shop, the manager of your local mall, etc.

3. Tell the other businesses located near yours about your plans and any impacts to parking or traffic that might result. Offer them an opportunity to participate, or invite them and their staff to attend.

3 Weeks Before Event

1. Double Check: Review your plan for the event itself. Ensure that staff are on board both in terms of knowing their responsibilities as well as being motivated to help you reach your event goal. Make sure that staff understand the goals of the event, that they are inviting clients and that they aware of their responsibilities at the event itself.

2. Double check supplies, retail and other needs. Ensure that you have ordered needed food items.

3. Contact local caterers or wine shops to see if they want to participate by providing you with a free or low-cost option in return for the ability to promote their services to clients appropriately at the event.

4. Keep Inviting People: If your budget allows you to send postcards or note card invitations, plan to send at least two. Send the first one 3-4 weeks before the event date and another approximately 1 week before the event. Be sure that you make RSVP, registration or other instructions and event details clear. Keep it simple; tell invitees something about what they can expect at the event, what they might win, and other details that would incentivize them to attend; focusing on one or two of the most compelling reasons.

5. Write a Press Release: Send a copy of your invitation and a 3-4 paragraph press release to your local newspapers and city publications alerting (and inviting them) to your event. If you are including a charitable aspect, be sure to state this as well as what your motivation for supporting the charity is and what your goal is.

2 Weeks Before Event

1. Triple Check: Supplies, equipment, food, retail, etc. should be completely determined and ordered by now, and most items (apart from food) should be on hand. Triple check your list and make any substitutions you need to in your plan for the event logistics or those things that will take place during the event.

2. RSVPs and Invitations: If you are holding an RSVP required event, check your list for early RSVP-ers. Formally responding to invitations seems to be becoming a lost art in our society, so do not assume that if someone has not yet confirmed their intention to attend that it means they do not want or are not planning to do so. Plan to make phone calls or send e-mails to key clients or other individuals you want to attend and extend them a personal "Hope you can make it!" invitation.

1 Week Before Event

1. Firm up responsibilities: Confirm M.C. (master of ceremonies), hostess and greeters as well as any other entertainment or special guests on the event schedule.

2. Layout a firm time line of how you want the event to flow, who will open the doors, how attendees will be greeted, ushered, who will take and retrieve coats, where supplies will be staged, etc.

3. Ensure that staff are on board, that the caterer and all other outside vendors confirmed, and all needed supplies and equipment are on hand or scheduled for the event.

4. Extend personal telephone and e-mail invitations to confirm attendees.

Day Before Event

Confirm with your staff and event partners – one more time – the time line and individual responsibilities. Make sure that everyone involved knows what time they need to arrive, and what time they will be staying until afterward (clean up and setting the space back to rights is everyone's responsibility, not just yours!)

At the Event

Make it your goal to collect e-mail and contact information for 100% of attendees. Plan a simple, natural-feeling way to collect the e-mail address, name, mailing address, and phone number (in that order of importance) for everyone who attends. Holding a drawing (or more than one) at the event is an easy way to collect contact information. Ensure that every attendee receives a flyer or postcard-sized bounce back offer to take away from the event along with their goodies, winnings, samples and purchases.

After the Event

Debrief with staff and partners: No event is ever planned perfectly, and no event runs perfectly. Things happen. Some are out of your control (like the weather) and some, well, just happen. Take time to debrief in a way that is honest but positive and supportive as well. It does not mean you have to candy-coat anything that went wrong or the failure of any individual who did not do what they should have. But the main goal of the debrief should be to get it right the next time, and to ensure there will be a next time by making sure staff are thanked for what they did and enthused to tackle your next event.

Follow Up

Within a few days of the event, be sure that every attendee receives a time-sensitive client appreciation bounce back offer from the salon via e-mail and/or direct mail. Thank staff and partners for their participation and support in writing, as well as any distributors or manufacturers who supported your event. Write a press release with results (and pictures, if possible) to submit to local newspapers and publications.

Social Site and Network-Based Marketing

With a nod to the consumer's increased awareness of the benefits of shopping locally in order to support the local economy, this is the perfect time for you to join (or start) a 'buy-local' initiative in your neighborhood or city. The math is simple: The majority of dollars spent at national chain or big box stores leave a community; the majority of dollars spent at local, independent businesses stay within the community. When consumers are educated about how their expenditures impact local jobs and the local economy, they often change spending behavior.

There are non-profit "Buy Local" campaign organizations that can provide your community with a host of resources including consumer-education materials to create this awareness within your community. In addition, when you take leadership in your community to support or initiate these efforts, you will promote your business to other local civic groups and businesses in an organic way, raising the status and reputation of your business within your community.

Join and become involved in a local Merchant, Business Park, Chamber of Commerce or Rotary organization. Reach out to other businesses that are in your physical proximity, or who serve clients with the same demographic characteristics of your ideal clients.

Even if you do not yet have a web site or any web building skills, you can easily create a Facebook page (or other social web site option) where you can promote your business to the local community and reach out to your clients with special offers at no cost to you beyond your time. You can use this marketing channel to demonstrate your salon's commitment to the community in charitable endeavors, show off the work of stylists in pictures, give tips to clients for seasonal looks or healthier hair and skin and speak to human interest stories of staff or clients – all in a way that your clients (or prospects) can connect to socially and emotionally, rather than giving a sales pitch.

Ding-dong!

The doorbell rings while you are making dinner and (reluctantly) you answer, opening the door to a total stranger who (you correctly assume) is there to make a pitch.

Despite your repeated attempts to (politely) say, "no, thank you," the salesperson (trained to 'overcome your objections' with at least 99 different scripts) continues to pressure, cajole, flatter and otherwise annoy you until you either give in and buy a little something or send them away with a firm rejection.

How do you feel afterward? Would you answer the door to this stranger again or would you pretend not to be home? Would you seek out the company that trained them in order to make additional purchases, thanking them for preparing the salesperson 'not to take no for an answer,' or would you craft a less complimentary message for this company?

While for the most part traditional marketing and advertising is comprised of overt sales and brand messages and a 'call to action,' when it comes to social media marketing, one of the keys to a successful strategy lies in the first word: Social.

While you can include overt marketing messages on your social marketing channels, your primary goal in using this media should be to further increase your web presence, letting customers and prospects know more about who you are (by sharing your values, principles, expertise, and creating opportunities for Word-of-Mouth marketing. Using social media marketing channels to facilitate 'hard sell' messages is a turn-off that will likely ensure your sites receive significantly less– not more– traffic.

Why? In social media marketing you are inviting your customers and prospects to engage with you on a more personal level. You are asking them to trust you enough for an introduction to their friends, family, co-workers and neighbors. How personal would you get with the salesperson at the front door? Would you send them on to annoy and bully your family and friends? (Of course not!)

When it comes to social media marketing for your salon, remember that this is not a traditional advertising or marketing channel. Before you set up a Facebook page for your salon or professional services, set up a Facebook page for yourself. Add "friends" and review their pages; chances are you will find that they are on Facebook primarily for social purposes and engaged primarily in social conversations. When it comes to your salon's social media marketing, use these channels in such a way that it is welcome in the lives of your readers. Craft messages that will be seen as an organic part of the conversation found in the 'News Feed' on Facebook, rather than blatant sales pitches. Use these sites as if you were invited into the living room of the reader for a visit; yes, you might talk about your business if asked to do so, but you would not try to sell them– well, anything!

One of the best aspects of social media marketing is that there is little monetary cost associated with its use; however, it can become a costly endeavor in terms of time, especially when this assignment is one added to a long list in the life of a busy salon or spa professional. Some 'how to' guides suggest that as much as 25% of your working time could be devoted to social media channels. While the time you need to devote to this aspect of marketing may vary, the point remains that to be effective, it requires that time be consistently invested in updating, blogging, adding photos to demonstrate your work, inviting people to events and providing follow up to questions and comments. This is a two-way dialogue where (to be effective) you need to hold up your end of the conversation.

Like any other campaign, your social media marketing cannot thrive without being nurtured. If time is at a premium for you, if you have never ventured onto the internet or if the idea of setting up a Facebook page or Twittering makes you break into a cold sweat, don't despair! Social media sites have created interfaces that can be managed by even a computer novice. If you are reluctant to try it yourself, you can readily find a high school student in your family or among your clientele aspiring to a future in the salon industry or marketing who would be thrilled to work for you for a couple hours each week, either to set up and manage your social marketing channels on an on-going basis, or to train you to take over. You may find that once you begin to experiment with social sites, it's easy to become addicted to the very real conversations that are occurring every day in the "virtual" world!

And remember, as you wade deeper in to viral marketing waters, use these channels to create customer love and referrals by sharing stories about your salon or staff that you would want to share in your client's living room and that readers will want to pass on to others.

January

bubble bath marketing—
"Calgon, take me away!"

If you are old enough to remember Calgon's long-running ad campaign, reading that phrase probably brought to mind the image of a woman with her hair up, closing her eyes and leaning back in a hot bubble bath, begging the suds to take her to a place of oasis and fantasy, an escape from her real life. We do not know what she wanted to escape from, but we were acutely aware that she was enjoying a rare moment of indulgence, pleading for complete transport to a better place.

"Bubble bath" marketing and client practices are rooted in the premise that a relevant, stimulating, engaging and indulgent client experience is powerful in attracting and retaining clients and increasing retail and service sales. Creating a client-experience that transports the client to a moment of escape or oasis is particularly relevant now, during this time of slow economy. So many of your customers have been negatively impacted financially and nearly all have experienced a significant amount of fear relative to possibility of job losses and other impacts of slow consumer and business spending. Haven't there been times lately when you wanted to spend a few moments escaping from the stress of reality?

As a salon or spa professional, creating "bubble bath moments" for clients should already be an organic part of your work; but often it is not, at least not in an intentionally constructed (and therefore more purposeful) way. Few businesses, even in luxury markets, approach their planned business model and day to day operations – each and every client experience – with the goal of creating an indelible moment of luxury and escape for the client. Creating positive, memorable client experiences is vital to ensuring that clients return, and is irreplaceable when it comes to asking for more frequent visits and client referrals.

In mid-2008, I needed to replace a vehicle. Dreading the experience that I expected, I visited three dealerships that had the type of car I wanted (a compact crossover); one luxury dealership and two more economical ones.

The luxury dealership paired me, after a short wait, with a sales person and we sat down to discuss what I wanted. Despite the fact that I told the sales person that I was just beginning to look at vehicles and really just wanted to test drive a certain car, he kept me in his office for about 30 minutes while (without my permission) the service department of his dealership did a once-over on my car which would be a trade in. After a lot of idle, unrelated chit chat, eventually I got to test drive a car, which performed to expectations but not beyond. Overall, a forgettable experience.

I next went to a Toyota dealership; I have owned a couple of Toyotas in the past and had great experiences with their performance and reliability. Once on the lot, I strolled for a couple of minutes and was soon joined by a sales person. This individual immediately put some obvious sales lines down to try to establish rapport, and within a few minutes we were on a test drive.

To detour the cliché car sales talking points, I asked him about himself and was not disappointed; he was more than willing to tell me a lot about his life and why he had taken a job at the dealership (it not only spared me a few minutes of hard sell, it showed me that this individual was all about himself, not me). From the beginning, it was clear that he missed the point where I said that he did not need to sell me on the Toyota brand, having owned Toyotas before; what I was looking for was a good experience at the dealership.

create indelible client experiences

Once back at the sales office I asked him to simply give me the dealership's best price on a certain model, stating emphatically that I was not a negotiator, either the price would be right and I would drive off with the car, or not. The sales person insisted that he could not work a quote up for me on the vehicle without running my credit and license; I objected several times, then eventually caved in because I thought that I really wanted the car. About 20 minutes later, instead of returning to me with a best price quote, which was what I had specifically requested, he asked what kind of a monthly payment I wanted. I asked at least three times for a bottom line price on the car, which I finally received. It was about five thousand more than I told him I had wanted to spend.

I asked for the immediate return of my license (which he still had in the back office) and had to ask, point blank, three times for it to be returned. Before returning it he actually insisted that he would "let me" leave for an hour in his personal vehicle to "think about" the purchase before he would return my license.

Incredulous at the blatant bullying strategy of this salesman and at this point livid, for a final time I demanded the immediate return of my license, stating that I was not going to make a decision that afternoon. He returned it – finally – but not after telling me that he was only going to be at the dealership for about another two hours.

In a final act of self-indulgence, he had the audacity to tell me I needed to make a decision immediately because he was going to leave early to go fishing. I pointed out to him that it would not matter; he would receive credit for the sale whether I came back when he was there or not, to which he replied that he wanted to be there to detail the car out for me. I left. Sad to say, this individual fulfilled my expectations for a car-buying customer experience, and ensured that not only would I never step foot in that business again, but that I would also warn anyone engaged in a search for a new automobile to avoid it all all costs. (To date, I have told at least 6 people not to visit that dealership, and why.)

who would you refer to?

Not even wanting to continue the process, but needing to replace my vehicle, I drove around the block and came back to a Honda dealership that was directly across the street from the Toyota dealership. I strolled around looking at some of the CRV models on the lot; to my surprise I was not joined by a sales person. Wanting to take one out for a spin, after about 15 minutes I entered the dealership and approached the nearest sales desk. I was greeted by a young man who asked how he could be of service. I replied that I wanted to test drive a CRV. Without hesitation, he picked up the phone and asked for a test model to be brought around.

A gray CRV appeared within a couple of minutes by the nearest door, the sales person gave my license a visual once over for validity and said, "Have fun!" Stunned, I said, "You're not coming with me?" and he replied, "No, I want you to be able to take the car out, see how it handles on the freeway, and test it out on your own." He walked me to the car, made sure I knew where the important features were, how to adjust the seat, etc., and off I drove. Alone with my own thoughts, I started to relax and tested the car without pressure.

After returning to the dealership, I told the salesman that I wanted to get a price on a certain model they had on the lot, that if the price was right, I would leave with it that day. Within about 10 minutes, he returned with a bottom line price. It was exactly what I wanted to spend (which he had never asked me) and was several thousand dollars below the MSRP and even below their online price.

Pleased that he had listened and given me what I had asked for, I said, "Ok, let's do it." It was that simple. Although I was pre-approved for financing with another company, the dealership asked my permission to do a credit check and see what their financing department could offer. Again, having begun to earn my trust and having made my experience painless up to that point, I agreed; and their financing department was able to offer me financing at a whole point less than my own financial institution. An hour or so later I was on the road home with my new vehicle, one customer experience that I have largely forgotten, one that I would never wish to endure again, and one customer experience I cannot wait to repeat.

Since that time I have sent at least six people back to that same dealership, to that same salesperson, to look at cars; from a neighbor who wanted to buy a used car for their kids to total strangers in the grocery store parking lot who approached me to ask about how I liked the CRV. I still carry that salesman's business card in my wallet, now a full 18 months later. I open his e-mails and direct mail pieces. I would not hesitate to send a friend, family member, or co-worker to purchase a car from the dealership or the salesperson. He created an indelible, positive client experience simply by treating me in the way he would want to be treated. He listened to what I said I wanted and then gave it to me. He took the pain out of the sales process. The two experiences were so completely, strikingly opposite.

This is not a reflection on either car's parent company; I would buy either again. It is a reflection of two competing businesses and the philosophies with which I now assume (based on these two experiences) they are managed. It is a reflection of two individuals who approach their job from opposing points of view.

While both receive compensation only if I purchase from them, one views his job only from the standpoint of what benefits him, immediately. The other knows that he will benefit far more by viewing his job from my point of view, from creating a client experience based on trust and a relaxed atmosphere rather than fear and pressure. I cannot wait until I need to purchase another car; if this experience is repeated, I will only be visiting one dealership for a long time to come.

Just as with the car dealership, the silver bullet to creating "bubble bath" client experiences in your salon or spa is not which products you carry or the price point of your products or services. The magic is in the personal client experience that you deliver, and in the atmosphere that you create through your communications, your furnishings, your ambiance – in the sights-sounds-smells of your salon – and most importantly, through your personal customer service. Each of these components is completely under your control and up to you to create. If you are not creating these components with purpose, then you are creating them inadvertently and you are leaving some of the most critical aspects of the customer experience to chance.

why it matters, more than ever

Despite both government and media telling us that "the recession is over," the fact is, the recovery is slow and has yet to make an appearance in some regions. The recession hit industries and services that rely on disposable income (and are not considered necessities) particularly hard. While clients still need haircuts, they find that they can take a couple more weeks of grow out before rebooking. More clients are experimenting with over-the-counter hair color. Fewer clients are able to afford massages and spa treatments.

The truth is that while the technical conditions of recession may be over, the impacts of the recession are still landing, and will be for some time to come. Jobs are still being lost, consumers are still cutting back on spending, and financial institutions are still tightening conditions for lending. No matter how fast recovery does or does not occur, many of the changes that occurred on the consumer landscape in the first decade of this century are here for the long term.

One aspect of consumer behavior that has changed can mean more business in particular for local retail and service providers. Consumers are more aware of and concerned with the local economy and the impact of how their expenditures support local jobs. With the prospect (or reality) of job loss ever-present in today's economy, reductions in income and resultant impacts to lifestyles, and the very real fears individuals have about their ability to support their families and meet financial obligations, there are comfort and indulgence-hungry customers near you that want to spend their dollars locally.

When economic conditions constrict, many advertisers shift the feel of marketing toward comforting, tradition-based and personal indulgence messages. Sales of comfort and indulgence items such as moderate and low cost wines, chocolates and other small indulgences not only hold, but gain ground. And with fewer disposable dollars to spend, consumers become much more aware of how – and where – they spend those dollars.

whose eyes are you looking through?

All of this is good news for small, independent businesses that can provide "bubble bath moments" in the form of products or services, social connections, local jobs and for businesses that give back to the community with support for local charities and by putting dollars back into the local economy.

People are also more "plugged in" than ever before; not only to news and information, but to events and online resources that give them an outlet to share their experiences and hear about the experiences of others who are experiencing similar joys or sorrows. Social sites like Facebook, MySpace and LinkedIn have blurred the lines between the professional and personal, allowing people to merge work, family and home. These sites allow consumers to interact with, and comment on products and companies in a way that is instant and powerful; they share recommendations and endorsements as well as warnings and complaints in a very organic, transparent way. Consumers have access to more information about your business and the services and products you provide than ever before.

Coupled with fear induced by a slow job market and tight economy, the social and familial connections provided by sites like Facebook have further fueled their growth as people reach out for the comfort of family and friends. And the shared communities that these sites provide turn virtual strangers into friends and acquaintances. It is easier and cheaper than ever before for a business of any size to create an online presence and to create community, conversation and collaboration online with clients, employees, peers, and other professionals.

Gear your marketing strategy, messages and annual plan to support these new realities and provide strong messaging to your customers and prospective clients about how your products and services provide moments of comfort or personal indulgence.

A complimentary scalp massage (or hand massage) given while your client is being prepared for hair services at the shampoo bowl might take just a few minutes, but it can create a moment of escape, personal care and indulgence for your client they will not receive anywhere else.

create addicts

As someone who spends anywhere from four to sixteen hours in a given day with my hands typing away or wrapped around a mouse, I can attest that a hand massage might be the single most relaxing, pleasurable add-on that you could provide to me in the salon. For your clients who work on the computer several hours a day or work in other ways with constant hand and arm motion, providing a "bubble bath moment" to relax their hands or arms creates yet another moment of personal rapport with the client, deepening your relationship with them as a salon professional and engendering loyalty – where else could they receive that kind of treatment?

A complimentary deep, aromatherapy-based conditioning treatment that leaves the client's hair silky smooth and smelling great costs you little in product or time. Since smell is one of the most powerful memory triggers, it also provides you with an organic way to introduce your client to products in order to support retail sales; you are giving the client a sensory experience that they will want to repeat at home.

one more example

A few years ago I was going through a very difficult personal time in my life. At the tail end of a painful divorce, I was about to go on a date for the first time. My stylist (Dawn Taylor, owner of Salon Bella Dea in Auburn, Washington) was shampooing my hair in preparation for a cut. Knowing that I lacked confidence and would want to look my best for this new chapter of my life, she asked if she could give me an eyebrow wax.

Not being one to take advantage, I started to decline. But before I could get the word, "no" out of my mouth, she had already applied the warm wax to my brows. She gave me an (amazing!) eyebrow wax because it was something she could do, from the heart, to personally help me as I ventured out into a new phase of life. She wanted to do something to make me feel more beautiful and more self confident. It probably cost her pennies in wax and almost no time, but even now, years later, this act created an indelible experience that can still bring grateful tears to my eyes. She showed me that she cares about me, as her client, in a way that transcends my haircut and color.   She gave this service as a gift to me out of the abundance of her heart.

Now each time I go in for a service, she jokingly asks (as she is applying the wax) whether I want a brow wax, and I laughingly say, "no." She made me an addict; to the brow wax, yes, but most of all to *her* as my stylist.

As you evaluate your clients needs individually, you can identify small random acts of kindness that will engender loyalty far beyond any cost of time or supplies expended.

If you begin to analyze the client experience in your salon or spa, you can create a long list of low-cost services and products to sample to customers to keep them coming back more often. Create memorable sensory experiences clients will want to repeat, that you can offer as freebies to entice new customers into your business, or provide as rewards for referrals or your most valuable clients.

January Event and Promotion Ideas

Unless you have a plan, January and February can be notoriously slow months in the salon and spa. Now that all of the holiday parties and the busy social season has passed, there can be a real post-holiday lull and you are not the only one left with a gap in your social life; your clients have one too, and they will welcome opportunities to get out of the house, mix with other people and keep those winter gray sky and cold weather blues at bay!

start a new monthly event: movie and makeover mondays

Movie and Makeover Mondays can be profitable for you while also providing a social outlet for you and your clients. This is a great opportunity to create cooperative and cross-marketing partnerships with other businesses that you can partner with throughout the year on events – from bars, restaurants or wine shops with TV/Video capabilities to caterers, party and event planners, independent sellers (or anyone else who wants to develop a strong "girlfriend" network and increase their client base).

Ironically, one of your strongest potential partners for this event (even though it may be mainly female-client-oriented) may be a local sports bar. While they typically cater to a more male-oriented base, there is a reason that so many bars have Ladies' Nights when girls get in for free: it is because male customers come out, in numbers, to meet them. Plus, a sports bar probably already has the video equipment you need for a movie night. Outside of football season, Monday nights may be slower; besides, football season is just about to end with the Super Bowl in early February – so a Sports Bar might welcome your approach now in order to help keep their Monday nights busy.

6-8 weeks before the first event

Begin handing out save-the-date business cards, flyers or post-cards and do a targeted mailing to those among your female clientele most likely to enjoy – and who most deserve – a night out with the girls. Build in an incentive for them to bring a friend (new to salon). Plan to repeat the direct-mail invitation and press for RSVPs 1-2 weeks prior to the event. As early as possible, post the date on your web site, Facebook and other social networking sites and put up flyers or posters in the salon.

Distribute copies of your flyer to local businesses and to the employees of your marketing partners. Send a copy of your event flyer and postcard to your local schools inviting teachers and other school district staff to the event. Send a copy to your local women's civic group and the PTA (Parent-Teacher Association) organizations serving your local schools and local MOPS chapter (Mother's Of Preschoolers). Join forces with a local women's fitness facility or a fitness, dance or jazzercise instructor, with area wine and martini bars, or with dinner preparation businesses and extend invitations to their customers and staff.

When creating invitations for distribution to businesses and organizations outside of your current clientele, your goal should be two-fold. You want to promote the event at hand, but you are also want to introduce your salon or spa to prospective clientele. Be sure that your materials are branded and tell something about the story of your business, what you offer to new clients, and above all, prominently display your contact information and hours of business.

Create special offers with all of your marketing partners to extend to all attendees, take appointment bookings and plan to do mini-makeovers, blow outs or cosmetics touch ups at the event. Create a plan for follow up (with another offer) after the event.

planning for the event

You will need a TV and DVD player to show the movie, and comfortable seating. Make sure you have enough space to set up a separate area where you can do demo hair and mini makeovers, as well as set up retail products for sale (if you are not doing the event in-salon). Choose a movie that "girlfriends" would enjoy seeing together, and partner with a restaurant or caterer to provide appetizers and drinks.

Decide ahead of time which services you will offer during the event, services for which you will be taking bookings, services for which you will sell packages (such as buy 5 haircuts, get the 6th free) and services that you will provide to each attendee in the form of a free consultation along with a 'prescription' service and product card to take home. Providing clients with prescriptive style and care recommendations is a great way to suggest both services and products that the client should purchase. It provides them with a tangible take-away piece and plants the seed for future service and product purchases.

If you will be offering consultations or mini-services, be sure that you have adequate staff on hand to perform these services and that you plan enough time for the duration of your event to accommodate this as well as the movie itself. Be sure that any collateral (such as a prescription card) that the client will be taking away from the event clearly features your salon's name and contact information.

before the event

If your event will be held in your salon or spa, plan your time line and set up the salon so that you are prepared to offer demonstrate color, highlighting, straightening, styling, make-up, massage, manicure or other services on a few client-models in order to demonstrate some hot looks or makeovers to attendees.

Determine whether you need to collect a cover charge to offset costs or in order to raise money that will be donated to a charitable cause. If you have partnered with other businesses to provide food, beverages, space or other supplies for fees, this will affect your overall event-cost for the evening and may mandate the need for an entry fee.

Do not be afraid to charge a cover fee for an event. Regardless of the validity of the principle, people sometimes view the value of an experience or product in proportion to its cost. They may perceive that a "free" event has no value (rather than realize that they were treated to a gift). But just because *they* did not have to pay for it, it does not mean that it was free. If you are holding a no-charge event or providing free services, be sure that you put the estimated value of the experience into a monetary value (as in, "complimentary mini-makeover, $25 value", etc.) on print collateral advertising for the event and in signage and on collateral provided at the event.

Determine which discounts or special promotions will be offered by your salon as well as your marketing partners to attendees. Decide whether you can gift something to attendees. Ask distributor sales consultants whether they can provide any manufacturers samples or trial size products, a gift basket for drawing, etc, and ask your marketing partners whether they can donate items to gift to attendees (this can also help boost the perceived value to the customer and counter negativity regarding any entry fee you may need to charge). Other vendors you might partner with include wine shops, a chocolatier, local deli or sweets shop, caterer, restaurant or bar.

Take bookings at the event, give attendees bounce back coupons and other take-away marketing collateral at the event including your business card, your menu of services and any incentives you offer for referrals or clients new to salon.

It is vital that you collect contact information for all attendees (e-mail address, address, name, etc.) in order to conduct follow up activities, send additional marketing offers, extend offers to book services, and send invitations to "the next one." Hold a drawing; one lucky attendee (or more) should win a free gift basket, product, service or free add-on service in January. Holding contests and drawings is an effective, low-key way to collect contact information from attendees and may make them more likely to give you permission to add them to your e-mail or direct mail subscriptions.

After the event, follow up by providing customized bounce back offers for all attendees for the services or products that were offered at the event, especially for those in which there was the most interest.

new year - new you!

Create "Re-New-Year, Re-New-You" or other New Year-themed packages of bundled or add-on services promoting new looks for clients such as cut with color change, or cosmetics, or salon plus spa service menu combination.

resolution helper

Help clients meet their New Year's Resolutions. Automatically enter them in a drawing for a free service in February when they write down their New Year's Resolution/s on a business card. Partner with a local gym, fitness, jazzercise or dance instructor to offer discounted, buy-one, get-one or other incentives. We are all more likely to keep our resolutions when we have a support system, so incentivize clients to refer a friend for this promotion. To help track results and continue momentum, set up a bulletin board in-salon or online for tracking progress against the resolutions that clients can update all year.

fruitcake exchange

In December, purchase inexpensive salon-branded products like pens, nail files, lip balm, mirrored compacts, t-shirts or tanks. In January, let clients exchange unwanted 'fruitcakes' (any poor-taste gift will do!) for branded gifts or manufacturers samples - or offer a discount on retail instead. Or create a fruitcake-exchange for clients where they can bring unwanted, un-returnable gifts to exchange for those of other clients (or to be donated to a local charity or thrift store).

sudsy sentiments

January 8th is Bubble Bath Day: Give a free salon-branded bubble bath product or another sudsy sample with retail or service purchase for everyone, for the first 50 responders, etc. Or cross-market with a local hot-tub seller to promote over-sized bubbly baths and salon services to both client groups.

winter chill-i

Set a date in mid-January to hold an official "Chili Day." Join forces with a local caterer, restaurant, build-a-dinner organization or similar business and cross market a special lunch or other event to both sets of clients to give away a free "Cup of Winter Chili" in the salon. Extend the spirit of winter chill-i by holding the event each week, or throughout the month. Promote a discount for services to "heat up" your client's look for the rest of the winter.

Gift, gift-with-purchase, hold a drawing, or even sell 'Chili Kits' you create with the pre-packaged ingredients clients need to create a great bowl of chili (in conjunction with a local caterer, grocery, deli, or dinner preparation business). Or gift 'Chili Kits' or caterer-provided chili to staff as an employee-appreciation event. This is a great opportunity to reach out to a local caterer, restaurant or dinner-preparation business to create the kits at little or no cost to you, in exchange for the cross-marketing opportunity to the other business, especially if you can provide a salon-branded item or product kit in exchange that they can gift or award to their clients.

Enhance the sense of shared community among your staff and clients by soliciting clients' best chili recipes and sharing them on your web site, your Facebook page, or as bag stuffers.

no pressure de-stresser

January is a perfect month for low-key social mixers. People need some time to enjoy themselves after the holidays without pressure and they are missing the busier social schedule that provided them with a constant stream of good times with family and friends. For a twist, set up a "mixer" with other stylists and salon professionals in your community to brainstorm solutions, share ideas and socialize. Or treat staff (and yourself) to massages or another de-stressing service.

55 and up

Winter can be an especially lonely time for seniors who may be stuck at home in the winter more so than they are in warmer months. Create an appreciation day for the 55 and up crowd in-salon. Or work with a senior services agency in your community to extend services to shut-ins and others physically unable to come to you. Check with your local senior community center or senior living communities to see whether they might welcome you coming on-site once a month to provide (paid) services to their senior clients, or coordinate with a local transportation company to find a way to get them out to the salon.

January Observances and Charitable Causes

Raise awareness for January month long observances like Crime Prevention Month, Prevention of Violence Against Women Month, and Self Defense Month, and related weekly observances like Women's Self-Empowerment Week (the second week of January) by creating cross or cooperative marketing campaigns with local crime prevention organizations, charities that support women and children, and facilities or professionals that provide self-defense, martial arts, personal safety or related instruction. Work with your marketing partners to create combined offer promotions and new client or referral incentives.

Consider a charitable event, fund raiser, or donated items or services for your local battered women's shelter or services office. Offer an add-on or retail discount for people who bring in food, clothing or a monetary donation for the local shelter.

Write a short press release for the local newspaper and your nearest city magazine detailing the money and materials raised, to whom it was donated, and how the public can donate to this organization. Include information about your next scheduled charitable event or fund raiser.

January Planning and Tasks

Working with staff and distributor sales consultants, order from manufacturers January-February promotions to support the client events and promotions you plan to hold in March and April.

Sales consultants continually offer you the ability to tap their expertise as well as corporate and additional manufacturers' resources and support – take them up on it! They may be able to provide personnel, supplies, manufacturers' samples or representatives to assist you for events or demonstrate products to customers in the salon. They may be able to provide you with support such as downloadable print collateral for postcards, invitations, or even for web and e-mail graphics. Your distributor should be an easy resource for you to utilize in obtaining marketing collateral and imagery to assist in promoting retail sales.

Put the finishing touches on January and February events including a Valentine's Day gift certificate sales plan. Begin publicizing Valentine's Day gifts and specials early in January (as well as any other February events and promotions). Put a healthy framework around your March events including your March 1st Men's Event (March 1st is National Beer Day!)

Order postcards, flyers, and artwork needed for February and March promotions, charitable endeavors and events. Layout plans for for March and April events now, identifying needed partners in order to have enough time to plan and publicize your coming promotions and events.

Communicate in January

Items to include in your email or print newsletter, web site and direct mail communications this month:

» Remind clients that this is the last chance for January events, expiration dates of promotions and RSVP deadlines.

» Solicit contest or drawing entries due in January.

» Introduce, pre-sell and highlight coming promotions and events for February, for Valentine's Day and all those occurring in the next 6-8 weeks (all the way into March). Give more weight in communications to those promotions that you feel will be the most enticing to customers. Make sure that those items are front and center in advertising, not lost in a long list of items.

» Alert clients to openings on the books for those whose locks are too long (and who forgot to pre-book).

» Create an offer to extend to those who might need help preparing for a special night out or those whom you have not seen in a while.

January Calendar / Suggested Communications and Tasks Schedule

SUN	MON	TUE	WED	THU	FRI	SAT
1st week of Month						
1st of January - Merchandise for January 1st of January – Begin collecting entries for January contests						
		Order from manufacturers retail promotions for products to support February-March-April marketing plans; design related signage			Send January Newsletter with coupons, announce contests and winners, new products and services, coming events, openings still on the books, events and promotions	
2nd week of Month						
Begin promoting and selling Valentine's promotions and Gift Certificates		Order in gifts, salon-branded items, impulse buy and other items for February			Write press releases for any events/results reporting or future events / charitable focus	
3rd week of Month						
		Layout plans for March events and promotions			Send January "last chance" promotions and openings on the books e-mail and/or direct mail	
4th week of Month						
Last day of January – Take down any January-only promotions Last day of January – Draw January contest winners						
		Order event supplies, postcards, gifts and salon-branded items needed for March promotions			Send February focus e-mail / direct mail	

January Worksheets

$_____ Retail Sales Goal

Promotions_____

_____

_____

_____

_____

$_____ Avg. Retail/Client

$_____ Retail Sales Results

$_____ Service Sales Goal

Promotions_____

_____

_____

_____

_____

$_____ Avg. Service/Client

$_____ Service Sales Results

$_____ Event Revenues Goal

Events _____

_____

_____

_____

_____

#_____ Attending Event/s

#_____ Apts/Booked at Event

$_____ Event/s Sales

$_____ Total Event/s Results

$_____ Charity/Fund Raising
Goal

Charity Events _____

_____

_____

_____

_____

#_____ Attending Event/s

#_____ Apts/Booked at Event

$_____ Charity Event/s Sales

$_____ Total Charity Results

January Marketing Summary

Marketing Partners: _____

_____

_____

_____

Marketing Collateral Needed (or Used): _____

_____

_____

Other Efforts:

#_____ Number of Clients New to Salon

%_____ Client Retention Rate (90 days)

  Retention Efforts: _____

_____

or % _____ Clients Rebooked at Appointment

$_____ Gift Certificate Sales

#_____ Contacts added to marketing / e-mail database

February

pet peeve your way to a plan

On February 10th, 2008 I was reading through a few e-mails for inspiration, a kick in the pants – whatever would connect with me the most. I clicked on an e-mail article titled "28 Days for the Heart," only to discover that the article is filled with great ideas that I should have started on at least 6 weeks prior in order to have implemented. I thought to myself:

> "Dear Author: Thank you so much for the great ideas that I will now print out and file away for next year, if I remember to look in ten months."

So, needing some practical inspiration for the day that would not leave me frustrated, I opened up a February trade magazine and read about Valentine's Day marketing ideas. I thought, Valentine's day is Saturday, let's see, um, today is Tuesday so if I hurry, I can construct a great marketing idea, lay out a campaign, send 2 postcards to my clients and 2 e-mail newsletters and order in the retail I need and get the gift certificates and partner with a restaurant to set up a cooperative gift package and sell through about 50 of these. In 4 days. Rrrrrright.

Opportunities missed make me crazy!

I understand the game; the game is to put out great articles that make people wish they were working with someone so creative and so smart. The game is to put out teaser articles that make people want to buy your publications. But if you are like me, the unintended consequence is that you are left frustrated because you realize you missed an opportunity. Personally, it leaves me feeling a little resentful, too.

I want ideas that I can use to build business now. I want ideas that I can use to revitalize my creative energies now. I want ideas to breathe some life and fun back into this slow economy NOW!

So here is what I propose. Brainstorm now on ideas to carry your salon or spa through to Father's Day. If it's already February, March is almost here so whatever you do in March has to be something you can organize and communicate quickly; but you are in good shape time-wise to plan for effective events and promotions in April and May.

Set aside designated time every month to plan ahead three months at a time to ensure that you will not be caught behind schedule when it comes to salon and spa promotions. Plan this time. Carve it out. Protect it. It is easy to become so busy with the moment to moment that creating an actual plan seems impossible; but it is the time spent creating the plan that can help ensure that you are not as overwhelmed with 'busy' moments in the months to come.

> plan 3 months
> ahead

march is employee spirit month

If you have salon- or spa-branded t-shirts or tank tops (or can get them made quickly), have staff commit to wearing them during work every day or at least every Friday in March. Purchase a few extra t-shirts to gift to your most valuable clients or give away with product in a free drawing. Use brand-ware to extend the presence of your business outside the walls of your salon or spa and into the community.

To raise employees' spirits, do things that are out of the ordinary for them in March. Leave anonymous notes complimenting their strengths. Share comments solicited from happy customers about their work or the difference they made in a client's life. Create a certificate-style award for each person in the salon or spa that highlights their personal strengths and hold spur of the moment huddles randomly throughout the month to give out each award in front of peers.

Or go big! Choose a day to close an hour early to hold an in-salon party including an actual awards ceremony. Or invite staff to a dinner or cocktail party at a local wine shop, bar or restaurant and hold your awards ceremony there for staff or expanded to include significant others. An annual employee awards show can also be a great alternative to holding an annual holiday staff event. More venues will be available and it will not put added strain into an already busy holiday schedule.

By the end of March, purchase brand-ware, gift and impulse buy items and retail products needed to support April's Jazz Appreciation and Client Loyalty and Stress Awareness promotions. Put finishing touches, schedules and deadlines around April's planned communications and tasks. Create signage, merchandising and point of sale displays to create the perfect atmosphere to help clients escape from stress and to reward and incentivize client loyalty. Work with staff to assign responsibilities. Identify and approach businesses with which you would want to partner for these events.

By the end of March, complete planning for Mother's Day retail, gift certificate, and service package promotions. Order in the supplies, salon-branded retail, and products needed for May's promotions. Set up a schedule for communications and begin to brainstorm about the signage, direct mail and other collateral you will need to promote May events.

april is jazz appreciation month

Continue to build your contact database by taking entries for a drawing to hold at the end of April; the winner might receive a Jazz CD or iTunes card, a customer-favorite retail product and a $10 gift certificate for service at your salon or spa (as a suggested gift package, you can go larger or smaller as your budget allows). Or, purchase 10 CDs or iTunes cards to award in client drawings by themselves or as part of gift baskets. If you are not giving Gift Certificates away with the music, be sure that you are at least including some kind of compelling bounce back offer in your prize package.

The point is not what you give away; the point is that with every entry you are collecting the name, e-mail address, phone number and street address of each individual who enters, and getting their permission to market your business and special offers to them. Once you start collecting e-mail and other contact data, don't just let that information sit on paper. Entering this data into your computer records should be a high priority so that you will be able to easily generate personalized mailings and mailing labels or to upload e-mail addresses to your e-mail newsletter hosting service. Also, having given you permission to market to them, they expect you to. Capitalize on the opportunity by providing every new contact obtained with communication as quickly as possible – before they forget about you!

12 Months of Marketing for Salon and Spa

Send a special "Jazz it Up" offer by e-mail to each person in your database. Turn up the music in your salon or spa just a little in April, or create music "Happy Hours" where the music is good and loud and where clients are treated to refreshments and happy hour pricing on add-on services or retail products. Create hair or skin care product "cocktails" for sampling.

Put the finishing touches, schedules and deadlines around May and Mother's Day planned communications and tasks. Complete ordering of salon-branded items, Mother's Day Gift Certificates, gift items, service and retail products.

If you have not yet extended your retail into cosmetics, as the calendar approaches Mother's Day and the summer's wedding and graduation seasons, it's a good time to begin. Start with a point of purchase lip gloss or lipstick display, eye shadows, mascara or nail lacquers; these items will make fantastic gifts for moms and daughters and will be easy to promote leading up to Mother's Day and into graduation and wedding seasons that follow. Treat stylists to a make-up application class via a local distributor or in-salon with manufacturers' representatives or other local educators. If you get stylists excited about makeup and knowledgeable enough to provide persuasive consultations and mini touch-ups following hair services, you will greatly increase the likelihood they will encourage clients to try and buy these retail products.

Create Mother's Day packages that bring in clients in pairs – mother-daughter, sisters, grandmothers,

design and sell
in pairs

mentors – every special woman. When you sell through gifts in pairs, you book two appointments in the time it usually takes to book just one, and chances are one of them will be someone new to your salon.

In April, reach out through e-mail and direct mail marketing to promote Mother's Day gifts and packages. Since you might only see clients once in the six weeks leading up to Mother's Day, begin marketing for Mother's Day no later than the first of April. Create a bag-stuffer so that each client leaves with a Mother's Day reminder and make sure you have signage displayed throughout the salon. Begin planning Father's Day promotions and packages, and brainstorming about the brand-ware, events and retail products you will need.

may is for moms, mates and multi-client packages

May. Mother's Day. Full-on Spring. Graduation is just around the corner and Cinco de Mayo (May 5) presents another perfect Happy Hour opportunity.

May is also National 'Date Your Mate' month which presents another obvious opportunity to go after clients in pairs. Find a restaurant to partner with for a cross-promoted, cooperatively marketed "date your mate" gift package. Create "two-fer" (two 'fer' the price of one) Date Your Mate packages which might include a cut and makeover in-salon in preparation for a two-fer at a restaurant that is partnering with you. Collect entries during May in-salon, in-restaurant, and online for a drawing to be held at the end of the month.

You can also create versions of your "two-fer" date packages to sell in-salon (or in your partner's establishments). Taking the pain out of date preparation might be especially compelling to your male clientele and it provides you with an opportunity to reach out to businesses with male-oriented client bases to cross-promote your packages (such as sports facilities, sports bars, golf or gentlemen's clubs, cigar shops, etc.)

As another suggestion, your winner's package could include gift certificates for two for the salon and for the restaurant, a movie, bowling or other date activities to honor the 'Date your Mate' theme. Make sure that everyone who entered gets a special offer – co-marketed with a salon-restaurant package offer or simply an offer on behalf of your salon. Complete preparations for Father's Day and begin marketing your Father's Day retail, gifts, gift certificates, and packages right after Mother's Day.

And as always, follow up by sending all participants a compelling bounce back offer.

February Event
and Promotion Ideas

It will take more than love to make February a business success, but Valentine's Day is an important – and can be a very profitable – holiday for your business. Order special Valentine's gift certificates, impulse buy items like pink and red lipsticks and nail lacquers, nail tips, nail files, candies and chocolates by early January in order to have them on hand to capture those 'lovin' feelings' from your clients! There are chocolatiers who have the ability to customize boxes or even the chocolates themselves, branding them to your salon or spa. Branded gifts make a much more lasting and memorable impact than generic ones do; do you want Godiva to get the credit, or you?

This month, show clients and staff where your heart is by sponsoring a blood drive or inviting a health care provider to give blood pressure checks in-salon for clients and staff. Or gather a group of volunteers to participate in an event at your local blood bank followed by a recovery mixer; to create a larger-scale event and reach more prospective clients, cross market this event with a restaurant, bar or wine shop.

who needs money anyway—
create cheapskate dates

Cheapskate Dates can be a great way to show the love to your clients! You can make a Cheapskate Date package into a thank you for your loyal clients or a gift package to be awarded in a drawing at the end of February. Partner with local restaurants, bowling alleys, concert halls, theatres or other date-destinations to create great date packages or offer multiple "date" prizes.

cheapskate offers

Create special "Cheapskate" promotions to run in conjunction with your drawings. Make sure to send all entrants (and everyone on your mailing list) the offers via mail or e-mail.

Create cooperative marketing offers with restaurant, bowling alley, theatre, chorale, symphony, or coffee shop partners; either purchasing gift certificates at half price or getting a buy-one, get-one offer donated. In this and in all joint efforts throughout the year, your strongest marketing partners should receive your strongest support when it comes to referring your clients to them via endorsements in your marketing collateral, distribution of marketing materials in your waiting area or at the point of purchase in your salon or spa, or verbally by you and your staff during the course of business. You will create even more incentive for businesses to partner with you, and to do so more generously, when they know that they are receiving a payoff in the form of new customers themselves.

Mix and match; if more than one organization will partner with you, create multiple or more valuable packages in order to share the love with even more of your clients. If a local symphony, choir or chorale is reluctant to donate tickets, consider purchasing an advertisement in their next program, offer to display their event posters in your salon or include their events in your newsletter or on your web site. Sponsor organizations like these both in order to attract the attention of their patrons and to incentivize them to donate tickets for your client drawing and gift packages.

Book the winning couple/s in for a glass of champagne (or sparkling cider), chocolates and a pre-date makeover. Make sure they walk out with a bounce back offer; chances are one of the guests enjoying the 'two-fer' package will be new to your business. This is your chance to impress them with the service, talent, fashion sense and the care with which they are treated by your staff. And it could be a chance to draw new male clientele into the salon or spa by showing them that your business caters equally well to them as you do to their girlfriends, wives and daughters.

Cross promote with your marketing partners to help them create "Cheapskate Date" packages to gift or award to their own customers. A pre-date makeover (or another offer) from you should be part of their prize packages. If you are partnering with a restaurant or bar, request that they display tent cards, salon-branded coasters or business cards throughout their establishment to promote your Valentine's Day offers. Extend your offers to employees who staff the businesses in proximity to your physical location, and to the employees of your marketing partners. They can be an invaluable source of referrals in addition to being prospective clients themselves.

two-fer

One obvious variety of a Cheapskate Date is a simple buy-one, get-one (BOGO) service offering. Almost any service or product which you can afford to extend at this margin, and that customers actually want, will work. If this is too difficult financially, then offer a buy-two, get-one free or a half off product on a second service or product when one of higher value is purchased (putting your discount to the client somewhere under 25%).

Partner with a local bar for a two-fer (two 'fer' the price of one) drink and appetizer or with a local restaurant for a two-fer entree or dessert to pair with your own offer. You can also partner with a local coffee shop for a buy-one get-one donation, a bowling alley, local theatre or community music group - the possibilities are endless!

updo, dine and ditch

Ask a local restaurant to participate in creating an Updo, Dine and Ditch Cheapskate Date. If they cannot donate a buy-one, get-one entree or meal gift certificate, ask them to sell you a gift certificate at half price. They will be getting a chance to impress prospective new diners during slow winter months in order to create new repeat customers of their own. If the offer is designed as a two-for-one for couples, two couples can even double date (and double your return when it comes to prospective new clients). Offer the gift certificates in a free drawing or as a reward or thank you for some of your best clients. You can even offer additional packages for sale.

love yourself

Why should couples have all the fun? Whether you celebrate Valentine's Day singly or as a couple, love yourself! Create special "Love Yourself" promotions around your most pampering services and retail products, or gift free salon-branded chocolates or aromatherapy products with retail purchases to clients.

insignificant other

An 'Insignificant Other' Event will take some work, marketing partners, and some creativity to execute. Partner with a local restaurant, wine shop or bar to host an "insignificant other" or "best-guy-I-never-dated" mixer. Just what it sounds like, this is a chance for clients to bring a non-date but great guy or girl out to a mixer at a local destination so they can both meet other great singles in the area. Collect contact information from all attendees with an at-the-door entry form which will also serve as an entry form in a drawing for a prize package to be awarded at the end of the evening.

Before the mixer, collect entries from your clients and hold a drawing for one lucky guy and one lucky gal to receive a pre-mixer makeover (remember, it's really all about the entries and gathering contact information for permission-based marketing). Create promotional offers for pre-event makeover bookings and a bounce back offer. Take bookings at the event and make salon-branded items (like shot glasses, event t-shirts, tumblers or mugs, etc.) or professional products available for sale.

After the event, send a bounce back offer via mail or e-mail to all participants (you collected their contact information before the event for pre-mixer makeovers and at the event for all attendees, and hopefully you ensured that your marketing partners did the same.

your really insignificant other

February 8-14th is 'Dump Your Significant Jerk Week' which gives you the perfect week to hold your 'Insignificant Other' mixer. If this event proves popular with participants, plan to repeat the formula during June's wedding season as a 'best-one-I-never-married' social event.

my heart beats for you

Partner with a local physician or other qualified health professional to set up a blood pressure education or blood pressure check reception in-salon or at a local wine shop, including education on the health benefits of red wine and chocolate. If you prefer not to tout the benefits of red wine, choose a non-alcoholic juice or health drink that also provides anti-oxidants, stimulates release of endorphins, boosts energy or provides other benefits.

the day the music died

February 3rd is the anniversary of "The Day the Music Died" which presents an opportunity to impress classic rock n' roll music lovers among your clients and prospects with a drawing for a free CD by one of the artists lost in the plane crash on that day in 1959 (Buddy Holly, Richie Valens, and the Big Bopper). Cater this promotion to the older generation; their service appointments or product purchases can serve as their entry. Or to make this more fun, hold a contest by having clients write down the names of songs they can remember by those three artists. The client with the most correct answers should win a special prize (but all entrants should receive a special offer). You can purchase low cost CDs from amazon.com or a local retail outlet for awards.

jell-o week

The second week of February is JELL-O* week. Give 12 and under (or all) clients a free cup of pre-packaged single serving jell-o at their appointment. Incentivize clients to bring their kids in to the salon during their schools winter break days off in February with a family cut package – and free jell-o, of course! In keeping with the catch phrase, "there's always room for JELL-O®," create "there's always room for…" services or products offered at low, jell-o cost pricing. Or, price one of your popular products or add-on services at the same price of a box of jell-o.

*JELL-O is a registered trademark of Kraft Foods

dum, dum, da-da, dum, dum, da-da...

Start marketing bridal packages now, especially if you want to book entire wedding parties in for their big day. Can you handle one more event? See May's "Bridal Show" notes.

February Observances and Charitable Causes

February is about affairs of the heart, and it's difficult to conduct a truly passionate affair if your heart is in trouble! Work with local medical professionals (such as family medicine, children's clinics, cardiac specialists, sports medicine clinics, or cosmetic surgeon's practices) who want to build business by creating cooperative or cross-marketed heart-health educational events or offers for both sets of clients. Working with a health care professional, create a list of heart-healthy tips, foods and activities and post them throughout the month on your web site, in your newsletters, on signage or bag stuffers.

Contact your local blood bank and offer to host a blood drive for them either in-salon or by bringing staff and clients to them; follow up with a reception where donors are rewarded with cookies and orange juice as well as with business cards and promotional offers. Consider offering free or half price color, hair cut or other service to everyone who gives blood, or hold a drawing for a free service for any of your clients who donate blood during February. Collect participants contact information and send them a special offer. Give gift certificates or BOGO coupons to the blood bank which they can give to donors at their site.

Follow up by reporting about your event (with pictures if possible) for submission as a press release to local media. Create a special discount or other offer for anyone who donates blood at your local blood bank during February. Post this offer in your e-mail newsletter, on your web site, on your Facebook page, and leave copies of this offer and your business card or menu with the blood bank.

February Planning and Tasks

Select from manufacturers retail promotions plus salon-branded items like nail files, branded sunscreen, lip balm, brushes, combs, water bottles, flip-flops, robes, towels, t-shirts and tanks or other items that can boost point of purchase and event sales or be used as gift-with-purchase items or as client gifts.

Design and print (or order) postcards, flyers, and artwork needed for March and April promotions, charitable endeavor and events.

Planning should be well underway for April and May events, including identifying needed partners and remembering that marketing and communications should begin no later than 6-8 weeks prior to events.

Finalize details for March and April events, promotions, contests and activities. Identify and capture needed marketing partners and delegate responsibilities. In March/April, remember to factor in spring break and the Easter-time holidays which provide another opportunity for family-based or kid's cuts (or teacher's cuts) promotions.

Communicate in February

Items to include in your e-mail or print newsletter, web site and direct mail communications this month:

- » Last chance for manufacturers promotions set to expire at the end of February

- » Solicit contest or giveaway entries due in February and announce January winners

- » Promotions and events scheduled during the next 6-8 weeks (all the way into April)

- » Alert clients to openings on the books for your clients whose locks are too long (and who forgot to pre-book), those who need help preparing for a special night out or those whom you have not seen in a while

- » Communicate loyalty and referral incentives to clients

- » Create and pre-sell winter break or spring break family haircut packages

February Calendar / Suggested Communications and Tasks Schedule

SUN	MON	TUE	WED	THU	FRI	SAT
1st week of Month						
1st of February - Merchandise for February 1st of February – Begin collecting entries for February contests						
		Order signage, event supplies and promotional materials for March promotions			Send February Newsletter with coupons, announce contests and winners, new products and services, coming events, openings still on the books, events and promotions	
2nd week of Month						
		Order in gifts, salon-branded items, impulse buy and other items for March			Write press releases for any events/results reporting or future events / charitable focus	
3rd week of Month						
		Layout plans for April events and promotions			Send February "last chance" promotions and openings on the books e-mail and/or direct mail	
4th week of Month						
Last day of February – Take down any February-only promotions Last day of February – Draw February contest winners						
		Order event supplies, postcards, gifts and salon-branded items needed for April promotions		Begin marketing spring and bridal packages and promotions	Send March focus e-mail / direct mail	

February Worksheets

$_____ Retail Sales Goal

Promotions_____

_____

_____

_____

_____

$_____ Avg. Retail/Client

$_____ Retail Sales Results

$_____ Service Sales Goal

Promotions_____

_____

_____

_____

_____

$_____ Avg. Service/Client

$_____ Service Sales Results

$_____ Event Revenues Goal

Events _____

_____

_____

_____

_____

#_____ Attending Event/s

#_____ Apts/Booked at Event

$_____ Event/s Sales

$_____ Total Event/s Results

$_____ Charity/Fund Raising
         Goal

Charity Events _____

_____

_____

_____

_____

#_____ Attending Event/s

#_____ Apts/Booked at Event

$_____ Charity Event/s Sales

$_____ Total Charity Results

February Marketing Summary

Marketing Partners: _____

_____

_____

_____

Marketing Collateral Needed (or Used): _____

_____

_____

Other Efforts:

#_____ Number of Clients New to Salon

%_____ Client Retention Rate (90 days)

 Retention Efforts: _____

_____

or % _____ Clients Rebooked at Appointment

$_____ Gift Certificate Sales

#_____ Contacts added to marketing / e-mail database

March

marketing for the single shingle

Very few things are more discouraging to 'solo artists' (such as booth renters, independent salon professionals, home-based business owners, consultants, estheticians, massage therapists; as well as stylists working to build their own clientele) than the realization that most business-building how-to books, articles and advice are written for those that have personnel and money to work with.

As someone who has worked for and with small businesses as well as shoe-string-budget non-profits for years, I understand some of the challenges faced by independent salon and spa professionals. You have boundless creativity, talent and drive, but often feel limited by a lack of time and monetary resources.

You are not alone. Regardless of size, to some extent, most businesses are limited in one way or another to initiatives that they have the time, manpower, equipment and resources to pull off.

As an independent salon or spa professional, you face all of the same responsibilities and challenges; but, unlike corporations with departments, specialists and support staff, you have to deal with every aspect and initiative of your business from planning to implementation and for everything from finance to marketing to the actual "work" all by yourself. So how do you, as a single salon professional, construct a plan that takes little or no money or support staff to implement, while still reaping the results of more clients, increased loyalty, more frequent visits and client referrals?

First, create a pattern for yourself. Set aside a block of time each month to look ahead for the coming three months. Thinking ahead gives you time to set dates, utilize e-mail or direct mail to promote your events and offers, purchase in retail or supplies needed, and to identify and recruit business partners to share costs and increase the size of your prospective client lists.

Second, stop thinking that you are limited to your own resources. There are many other

stop resource –limited thinking

'solo artists' and new small business owners who would welcome the opportunity to build business faster by working with you.

When so many of the 'dot coms' went bust in the 1990's, many entrepreneurs found themselves out of jobs and starting over. The small businesses and start ups they formed helped to get the economy moving again. Now in a post-recession, slow, job-starved economy, people who have lost jobs are once again turning to new home-based and entrepreneurial start up business opportunities to replace their income or while in between corporate jobs.

Some women who stayed home previously or chose to leave the corporate world for more flexibility are now working part time to contribute to the household as massage therapists, exercise instructors, and independent jewelry, jeans or other product sales. Self-employed solo artists themselves, many will welcome opportunities to work with you to provide more services to both client lists. Additionally, many of these enterprising women chose sales as a profession because they already have a wide sphere of influence. They may already be linked in with private and public school teachers and staff, PTAs, youth organizations, corporate groups, civic groups, support groups, churches and other organizations which will enable them to provide you with valuable referrals and large contact lists for cooperative marketing.

Other service and luxury businesses that rely on consumers so-called "disposable income" are also feeling the pinch and will welcome opportunities to share costs, co-sponsor events, and share contacts for cooperative and cross marketing efforts. Some of the businesses you might approach include spray-tanning salons, spas, cosmetic medical or dental practices, chiropractic offices, massage, fitness facilities, weight loss specialists, personal coaches party planners, etc.

Any non-competing business or independent professional whose 'ideal client' is a close match to yours in some way presents a potential opportunity for you as a marketing partner. Create goodwill among potential business partners by extending a deep discount or

---
be an asset to your partners
---

an occasional free service to owners, and extend generous offers to their employees. They will be better able – and so much more willing – to refer customers to you when they have experienced your talent, customer service and passion for your craft on a first-hand basis. And when a partnering business is sending new clients your way, be sure to thank and reward them; nothing reinforces desired behaviors as much as a gratifying thank you reward!

april is customer loyalty month

You can create a rewards program for loyal clients even if you are a one-man-show. Offer a discount or free add-on mini service as an incentive for the client to re-book at the end of each appointment. If you plan to provide a reward based on number of visits or dollars spent, create punch cards on your own computer designed to fit on a business card, and print them out on pre-perforated business cards (available at any office supplies store).

Or create a design (on your own or working with a local graphic designer) and order cards from a professional printer online at a low cost. For optimum cost efficiency, modify your professional business cards so that the back side of the card serves as your punch card, appointment reminder, or carries a special bounce back offer from you.

Your clients have many choices when it comes to salon and spa services. Let them know that you do not take them for granted by taking the time to thank each and every client with a thank you note or e-mail, text message or even a note on their Facebook page. If you can, purchase branded pens, rulers, nail files, lip balms, or other small personal items that clients will receive as a gift-with-retail purchase or as a thank you gift from you in April.

make may pay

May is full of dates which lend themselves to pairs and group offers. From Mother's Day to prom to graduation to the coming wedding and anniversary season – now is the time to construct and market mother-daughter, sister-sister, or girlfriend group packages for formals, updos, manicures, makeup parties and more. Business partnership opportunities abound in May – from party planners to restaurants, formal rentals, limo rentals and more.

love is in the air in june

Wedding season is almost here! Before June arrives, construct a bridal package cosmetics and hair special, a massage-relaxation special, a mother-daughter, mother of the bride or another bridal party offer.

Contact local wedding planners, formal rentals, limo rentals, bakeries, and local wedding and reception facilities to create cooperative and cross marketed offers. Partner with an exercise or fitness instructor to create 'get in shape for the big day' package offers that include getting the body as well as skin and hair in shape.

Promote the services of your marketing partners to clients who may be getting married (or have family or friends slated to take the plunge) and be sure that your clients mention that you sent them. You want your marketing partners to know how valuable your support is to them, and you want to be sure they are incentivized to do the same for you.

Create a flyer or brochure with your wedding services packages, special offers, or salon menu that can be mailed or e-mailed to clients or prospects. Send a flyer to area wedding planners, wedding and reception facilities and formal or limo rental businesses along with copies of your business card. Once again your business card can do double duty with a pre-printed offer right on the back of the card. Or go slightly larger, and order a folded "tent" style business card that contains enough extra space for you to print up all your bridal package offers, or a mini service menu.

March Event
and Promotions Ideas

An observance like National Beer Day (March 1st), makes March the perfect time to focus on men; and specifically to focus on getting more men into your professional life and into your salon or spa!

Stylists, spend this month making sure that male clientele know they are in the right place when it comes to getting their hair cut and cared for. Skin estheticians, focus on educating male clientele (and the women who love them) about their particular skin care needs, suggesting products appropriate for blemish prone or sensitized skin, or skin damaged from shaving or the elements. Massage therapists, emphasize the stress relieving and resultant health benefits or benefits for athletes that massage provides.

Make it your goal this month to seek out and cross-promote with at least three male-client-oriented businesses such as sports bars, fitness centers, martial arts, sports leagues, local military bases, outdoor sportsmen or hunters clubs, etc.

smile, it's happy hour!

When it comes to "Happy Hour" in the salon or spa, there are many ways to craft a new repeating, regularly scheduled event designed to make clients feel good about coming in, coming back, and bringing co-workers and friends with them – from the moment they enter your salon. Your Happy Hour should be crafted not only to make clients happier but also to make you happier; design Happy Hour offerings to help fill up the books during slower hours, promote new services and products, promote retail sales and add-on services, promote filling the books for new stylists, etc.

While the mind naturally goes to the idea of alcohol when you hear the term 'happy hour,' it doesn't mean that your Happy Hour has to be intoxicating per se – so don't dismiss the idea out of hand. If you can serve alcohol but worry about clients driving afterward, develop a Sangria recipe unique to your salon; you will cut some of the alcohol content without losing a drop of taste or the spirit of the event.

If you would prefer to (or must, due to state or local regulations) go non-alcoholic, keep the spirit alive with "mocktails" for client consumption and "hairtinis" or "skintinis" (special product cocktails for the hair or skin). Partner with a nearby natural foods store, deli, restaurant or juice bar to help create beverage offerings; or, create a co-sponsored Happy Hour for all clients (preferably at your salon, or experiment with a travel case and provide impromptu mini-makeovers for hair, skin, make-up or nails in your partner's establishment).

No matter where you celebrate Happy Hour, ensure that the collection of attendees' contact information and a bounce back offer are part of the mix. If possible, hold a drawing each week during Happy Hour for one lucky attendee to win a service or product gift basket.

However you construct your Happy Hour, make it a special time in your salon (in contrast to what occurs during your regular hours). Happy hour can be a chance to turn up the music and let your clients get a groove on. Include referral or bring a friend rewards, spot-prize drawings and contests, and even games, cards or entertainment.

more happy hour options
weekday-relaxer, weekend-ready

Create a Friday 2-6 PM 'date prep' or 'de-stress' Happy Hour for clients to get ready for a night out with a special someone, or get ready to go out with the girls (or the boys) while they relax for an hour or so with a glass of something. This can be a great way to let go of the stress of the week and get in the right frame of mind to relax during the weekend. Even if they are not going out, it's a great way for clients unwind after a long stressful week.

gift-wrapped clients

Create a Happy Hour package with free beverage that features services designed to "gift-wrap" clients for the evening such as a cut with color highlights or blowout and style plus mini-facial and cosmetics at a special package price (or just a blowout and style with cosmetic touch up for a quicker turn). Don't miss out on the opportunity to send styling products and cosmetics home with your clients - offer special Happy Hour pricing on retail products as well!

book builders

Hold your Happy Hours during what are normally slower times on your books during the week (such as weekday afternoons) to plump up bookings during those hours. Hours in between the lunch and dinner rushes may also be slower hours for restaurants as well; partner with a local restaurant to provide snacks or food or beverage coupons for distribution in the salon or spa in return for the opportunity to gain cross marketing referrals by extending their marketing collateral and special offers to your clients.

happy hour how-to, must-haves and menus

A true Happy Hour event or offer will have an aspect of social appeal. Give clients a reason to come to your salon or spa beyond their regular appointment (more frequently) and to bring friends with them. As you begin to plan, first ask yourself, who do you want to come to Happy Hour? If the answer is "everyone", then you aren't being realistic and are not likely to construct an attractive Happy Hour. Identify types of 'ideal' happy hour clients from larger subgroups within your clientele, or from your target market (the type of clients you most want to attract); such as:

» Single or married working professionals for an end of day or end of week decompress or prep for night on the town

» Stay-at-home or soccer moms and dads who are dying for and deserve a few minutes to themselves

» Sports oriented, blue collar, or other general male-oriented groups

» Senior citizens

» Boomers

» Male clients

» College students and young adults

» Girlfriend Groups

You can see why setting up a target group is important; what appeals to one generation or group vs. another can vary widely, from what they want done to their hair to what they want to drink to the music they want to listen to. It may be as simple as pleasing your staff and attracting individuals with some of the same demographic characteristics that they have, or by pleasing an employee group from a nearby business, etc.

The menu must include something yummy for the client; something that makes them – well, HAPPY! Find a restaurant to partner with so that during happy hour at the restaurant or bar patrons receive a business card with a Happy Hour offer from your salon; and during your Happy Hour, clients receive a special incentive to go to the restaurant.

If other businesses near you are interested, create a bigger, combined Happy Hour experience for clients and share costs and contacts for a cooperative marketing effort.

happy hour (brand) extensions

Order salon-branded coasters and gift them to local bars or restaurants that have happy hours. Their alcohol distributors sometimes provide them with free coasters; why not substitute those with coasters that draw attention to your business or to your services as a stylist, massage therapist, esthetician, or other industry professional? An average coaster is almost twice the size of a business card, so it should be no problem for your design to incorporate a referral reward or new client offer, upcoming special events, or a special, compelling offer for people who bring the coaster in to your salon or spa.

extensions of your brand, with a twist!

Order salon-branded coasters with your contact information, Happy Hour details or offer on them to use as bag-stuffers in the salon or for when you offer water, coffee and other beverages in the salon. You can even distribute coasters as business cards within your community and ask your marketing partners to use them or distribute them at the point of purchase to advertise your Happy Hour and services.

on the flip side

Your "coaster" (which can also be used as a business card, bag stuffer, or other advertising medium) has two sides. One of the first rules of marketing is: Do not waste the flip side of any marketing piece! The flip side of your coaster can do double duty and include an area for people to give you contact information; or, you can use the flip side to list other offers, a brief version of your menu, a client testimonial, or special features you offer in your business, such as special equipment, trendy popular services, TV with sports, news or other interests or Wi-Fi connectivity.

Your Happy Hour does not have to be alcoholic, but if you are going with an alcoholic beverage, have safeguards in place. Make sure you know, first and foremost, what the regulations are in your city/county/state for serving alcohol. There may be different regulations for serving alcohol at no cost than there is if you have a cover charge or charge per beverage. If you are going to incorporate alcoholic beverages, remember that most clients will probably be driving from your location to their next destination, so do not over-serve and be sure to incorporate food as well. If a client arrives noticeably pre-lubed or you believe that you have a guest who is experiencing a problem, have a plan in place and procedures for arranging transportation and safely delivering clients home, or for summoning medical or other attention if necessary.

st. patrick's day

If you don't want to make Happy Hour into a regular gig, create a St. Patrick's Day version on or near March 17th for a social mixer and retail blowout for clients.

luck of the irish

Irish or not, give clients the opportunity to enter to win something this month. Depending on local regulations, create a gift basket with a pint or two of a favorite regional micro brew (or root beer) and 'a pint' (mini or full-sized) of retail products to support your Beer Buzz or St. Patrick's Day promotions. Or, partner with a local restaurant to provide a free cocktail to clients. Make sure all entrants receive a special offer from you.

beer buzz!

March 1st is National Beer Day. Hold a Beer Appreciation event targeting male clientele with a special offer. From March 1-7th, offer presold packages of haircuts to your male clients of buy-3, get-1-free haircuts, or a presold take $3 off 4 haircuts card (either offer must be used within 90 days). Make this offer available again once each quarter to those that bought them during the original offering period.

Give away a free beer (or root beer) to male clientele and to any clients who purchase a male hair or skin care retail product.

Hold a special Happy Hour just for the boys (in accordance with regulations in your area for alcohol). Cross promote to area martial arts, fitness, sports, or other male-oriented businesses.

Partner with a local watering hole and turn the table on the traditional '"wet t-shirt'" contest. Challenge male patrons to participate in a "shave off" and use your best skin care products (or a sampling of men's shave products) to determine which products provide the softest, smoothest finish (it would not hurt to have a couple of gorgeous girls there to serve as judges).

inside and out

March is National Nutrition Month. Partner with a nutrition expert, chef, restaurants, or build-a-dinner businesses to offer clients great tasting, nutritious recipes or offers from your partner businesses. The goal should be to cross promote and share contacts, increasing the marketing exposure and client base for all. Partner with a dietician or chef to offer a seminar or classes to clients on healthy eating and diet. Extend your marketing reach and partner with a local jazzercise or fitness instructor too, touting the benefits of exercise.

inside spirit-wear

March is Employee Spirit Month. Design and order salon-branded t-shirts, aprons or other clothing suitable for employees to wear in the salon. Give salon-wear to employees and request (or require) that it be worn on Fridays, to special events, or every day.

Design and order cute, clever, funny or poignant salon-branded t-shirts, water bottles, nail files or other branded items for retail sale, contest giveaways or client gifts. Collect client data and award salon-branded gifts to drawing winners or give them as rewards for new client referrals.

employee spirit month

Hold an in-salon contest and give recognition awards to co-workers or clients who exemplify the spirit you want in your salon. Partner with a massage therapist to give mini-massages (and take bookings) as a surprise treat for staff and clients. Create a combined salon or spa service and massage bounce back offer for April. Connect your partner businesses with a massage therapist to provide mini-massages to them or to their employees.

March Observances and Charitable Causes

March is National Nutrition Month. It's about health and well-being. Its a great time for clients to resolve to start getting their bodies, skin, and hair in shape for summer. Create partnerships and cross-promotions with local dieticians, take-and-bake pizzerias, dinner-preparation and other similar businesses. Partner with restaurants that offer healthy meals and create offers for their clientele highlighting how your services and products improve the health and well-being of and nourish hair, skin or nails. Partner with local fitness, martial arts, yoga and other providers to create complete body well-being cross promotions and packages.

The third week in March is 'Wellderly' (Well Elderly) Week. Create a promotion for local seniors designed to enhance hair, scalp, skin or nail health. Coordinate with local senior social services regarding senior needs and volunteer or support local low-income senior charity efforts by giving a discount to clients who donate food or clothing to local senior services organizations.

Local churches or your city's rotary organization may provide occasional practical support to seniors or shut ins by performing yard work, chores, or handy-man tasks. Get involved by volunteering, or raise awareness, funds and additional volunteers from among staff and clients.

National Nutrition Month is a time to be aware of those less fortunate in our society who cannot always eat healthy, balanced meals. Consider a fund raiser or charity event (such as a Happy Hour with cover charge, or donate proceeds from retail sales) to benefit your local homeless mission, women and children's shelter, or low-income senior services providers.

March Planning and Tasks

Select from manufacturers March-April retail and back bar promotions in light of the events and promotions you will conduct in April, May and June.

Design and print (or order) gift certificates, postcards, flyers, and supplies still needed for April, Mother's Day, and for any other promotions or events coming in the next 6-8 weeks, all the way into June.

Identify businesses with which you can cross-promote for Mother's and Father's Day, establish partnerships and begin to identify and delegate responsibilities. Complete April planning, confirm partnerships and assigned responsibilities in terms of events, promotions and marketing.

Set target goals, set up a way to track and show results, and be sure that staff are on board and incentivized to support retail and gift certificate sales for Mother's Day and Father's Day (and any other appropriate activities planned for May-June, such as bridal business, etc.).

Communicate in March

Items to include in your print or e-mail newsletter, web site and direct mail communications this month:

» March-April events, promotions, charitable activities and contests

» Special interest items such as sentimental or humorous 'behind the chair' anecdotes, special achievements and education of staff, photos from events or great styles, makeovers, etc.

» Let clients know which promotions expire in March and what products are coming new to the salon in April

» Begin marketing for Mother's and Father's Day gift certificate sales by the end of March

» Solicit contests or drawing entries due in March and announce February's contest winners

» Use e-mail to help fill openings on the books by letting clients know of open time slots or cancellations, following up with clients who did not re-book at their last appointment, soliciting bookings for clients who have a special date, interview or another occasion to prepare for, etc.

March Calendar / Suggested Communications and Tasks Schedule

SUN	MON	TUE	WED	THU	FRI	SAT
1st week of Month 1st of March - Merchandise for March 1st of March – Begin collecting entries for March contests						
		Order from manufacturers retail promotions for products to support April-May-June marketing plans; design related signage			Send March Newsletter with coupons, announce contests and winners, new products and services, coming events, openings still on the books, events and promotions	
2nd week of Month						
		Order salon-branded thank you notes for April's customer loyalty initiatives			Write press releases for any events/results reporting or future events/charitable focus	
3rd week of Month						
		Begin promoting April events and sales of Mother's Day Gift Certificates; layout plans for May promotions			Send March "last chance" promotions and openings on the books e-mail and/or direct mail	
4th week of Month Last day of March – Take down any March-only promotions Last day of March – Draw March contest winners						
		Order event supplies, postcards, collateral, gifts and salon-branded items for May contests	Begin marketing spring and bridal packages and promotions	Send April focus e-mail / direct mail		

March Worksheets

$_____ Retail Sales Goal

Promotions_____

_____

_____

_____

_____

$_____ Avg. Retail/Client

$_____ Retail Sales Results

$_____ Service Sales Goal

Promotions_____

_____

_____

_____

_____

$_____ Avg. Service/Client

$_____ Service Sales Results

$_____ Event Revenues Goal

Events _____

_____

_____

_____

_____

#_____ Attending Event/s

#_____ Apts/Booked at Event

$_____ Event/s Sales

$_____ Total Event/s Results

$_____ Charity/Fund Raising Goal

Charity Events _____

_____

_____

_____

_____

#_____ Attending Event/s

#_____ Apts/Booked at Event

$_____ Charity Event/s Sales

$_____ Total Charity Results

March Marketing Summary

Marketing Partners: _____

_____

_____

_____

_____

Marketing Collateral Needed (or Used):

_____

_____

_____

Other Efforts:

#_____ Number of Clients New to Salon

%_____ Client Retention Rate (90 days)

  Retention Efforts: _____

____

_____

or % _____ Clients Rebooked at Appointment

$_____ Gift Certificate Sales

#_____ Contacts added to marketing / e-mail database

Elizabeth Kraus • 12monthsofmarketing.net

April

where the clients are

This has happened to all of us at one time or another; you were in a conversation with a client, co-worker or friend who presented you with a problem or even asked outright for you to help them think of a solution. However, once you began to offer suggestions they switched quickly into "nope, can't do that" and "that won't work" absolute negativity mode, and within a few minutes you shut down the creativity feeling almost bruised by the way your suggestions or ideas were eliminated like so many ducks shot in a pond. You left the encounter with a strong suspicion that they would rather wallow in their misery than actually try to do something to solve the problem.

What about you? Are you wallowing? Are you in a place where you can identify the things that are holding you back professionally or the areas where your business needs to grow? Is the prospect of doing something new, taking risks and changing the way you have "always" done things something that scares the bejeepers out of you, or do you welcome the turbulence of change because of the corresponding opportunities for adventure, variety and trying new things?

If you are waiting for things to get back to "normal" post-recession you are in for a long (read: forever) wait. News flash: This is the new normal. Gone, at least for now are the days when consumers had the confidence to live paycheck to paycheck (knowing that another paycheck was always coming in), spending freely and indulging themselves whenever they desired.

Some salons have seen female clients extend the time between routine hair maintenance services from six to eight or even ten weeks (or more), taking on their own hair color and purchasing care and treatment products formerly purchased in the salon or spa from retail stores. Clients need lower cost hair cutting services for children; families have to make every dollar count.

In the spa and luxury services segment of the industry, the disparity between the old normal and the new normal is even greater. Some spa clients have stopped coming altogether; others who used to visit weekly are now just coming once a month or once a quarter.

How much can you allow business to slow before you have to take on a second job or leave the industry altogether? What are you doing to create a new normal of your own that transcends economic factors? What are you doing to take back control of your business, growth of your client base, retail sales and income?

Salon and spas are natural settings for themed event and promotions. You have the ability to tailor packages, products and incentives for nearly every holiday and major life event – from new jobs to new babies to graduations to weddings to anniversaries to 'girlfriend' outings or dates. You see clients at a frequency to easily provide them with ever-changing merchandising displays and seasonal and personal gift suggestions. The coming summer months present exciting opportunities to flex your creative marketing and styling muscles, and create some buzz for your business.

> create your own
> new normal

may

Get out of the box (of your salon or spa) and go to where the clients are to promote Mother's Day gift certificates and package offers. Take copies of your business card, menu or special offers to area day cares, to the offices of private schools, and to the offices of your local public school administration. Get involved in your local PTA organization, your local Soroptomist's club, neighborhood merchant organization or city chamber of commerce.

If you look beyond the doors of your salon, you will find countless other businesses in your area that have concentrations of women, women who likely represent some segment of your target clientele. Women who network and socialize and refer friends to their favorite stylists, and who purchase countless home care products for themselves and their families.

june

Weddings (and anniversaries) and graduations; no stylist, nail or cosmetics esthetician who wants to be busy should be bored in June. To market bridal party offers, hold classes for a girls-day-out bridal brunch and tutor bridal parties in the best ways to achieve and preserve their looks on the big day, apply makeup, and style easy updos.

Invite a local party planner or caterer to hold a class for clients to give advice about how to throw great anniversary or graduation parties (and simultaneously market their services to clients who prefer not to bear the responsibility).

Partner with a caterer or local bar or restaurant to provide expertise and teach clients how to create mixed drinks, appetizers and other easy, delicious party fare for summer get-togethers. Make sure clients receive compelling retail and service offers for the day of the wedding, anniversary, graduation or summer party as well as a bounce back offer. If you can connect a caterer or party planner with some of your clients for an event, ask them to distribute a combined offer at the party as well as their own business cards to attendees.

always include a bounce back

father's day

Begin promoting product and service packages for Father's Day gifts by May 1st. Craft packages and certificates to be sold in duos (father-son, brothers, friends, couples, etc.), so that you will book two appointments rather than one upon redemption. Feature a Father-Daughter duo package that includes retail products 'for him' and 'for her.'

Even if you have mainly female clientele, you can still create retail gift baskets including products for men such as shaving, scalp, and skin care products and gift certificates. While sales of men's grooming and other personal care products have increased exponentially over the last decade, the vast majority of male grooming products are still being purchased on their behalf by women.

Partner with a local sports bar or sports activities facility and create gift certificate duos that include service at your salon and a round of golf, game of bowling, bucket of balls at the driving range or batting cage, etc. Partner with a local sportsman's club or retailer and create a package with hunting or sporting goods (or gift certificate) as well as men's skin care products and gift certificates.

july

Most communities have street fairs, festivals, parades and community events that give you the chance to 'set up shop' right on main street. Take advantage of community events and do some street marketing; you do not have to be in the salon to sell retail, demonstrate your skills and promote your business. Hand out business cards. Sell (or give away) salon-branded combs, nail files, water bottles or lip balms. Rent a booth, schedule and prepare models and do blow outs and styling, mini-makeovers, manicures, massages, demonstrate skin or hair treatment products and lotions, sell retail and take bookings. Hold drawings and award prizes, being sure that each one includes an irresistible bounce back invitation redeemable in your salon or spa.

august

Plan now to reach out to family and school markets with group rates for families and special rates for educators, the PTA and all school district personnel. For more, see August's ideas on the back-to-school student, teacher and family markets beginning on page 153.

April Event
and Promotions Ideas

April is Stress Awareness Month, and in the current economy stress is something we are all keenly aware of in our own lives as well those of our staff and clients. Life has never moved so fast, been so full of uncertainty, economic turmoil, sliding markets, job-starved communities and the continuing effects of the recession of the last decade. It is important to recognize the causes of stress in our lives, reduce them where we can, live more healthy and happy, and indulge appropriately in order to counter it!

April is also Client Loyalty Month which makes it the perfect time for you to design and implement incentives to promote and reward loyalty among your clients.

implement a new program
to boost customer loyalty

Nothing is healthier for your business and does more to alleviate professional stress than cultivating a healthy, loyal client base. Retention and loyalty initiatives may require the investment of time, supplies or money on your part; however, it can cost up to 5 times or more to gain new clients than to retain current clients.

The steps you take to ensure that clients will return and books remain full are worth the effort. Take the time to evaluate a client's experience from the phone call to book the appointment through to the end of their visit, evaluating each aspect of the customer's journey through your business. Even if your area of the salon consists only of one station, you still need to evaluate your client's experience at each touch point and you may need to lobby for changes from staff or persuade peers to help improve the experience.

- » How does the entrance and waiting area look? Is it clean? Is it obvious that this is where clients should wait?

- » Are furnishings adequate, attractive, in good repair and comfortable?

- » Are clients greeted? Are they told how long their wait will be and offered a beverage or snack or something to read? How long do your clients wait on average?

- » When you bring the client to your station, do you take the time to speak with them personally before getting down to business?

- » Do you conduct a good assessment of the client's hair, scalp, skin or other needs, really listen to what they want, and then propose additional services to improve the health of their hair or skin?

- » When you are performing your services do you tell clients about the products you are using and why you chose them?

- » Do you make clients aware of hair, scalp or skin issues they may not be aware of, including products or services which could bring them relief? Do you provide prescriptive-style recommendations, including usage?

- » If a client comes to you at a time they are struggling personally, do you find a way to go the extra mile with free add-on service or sample?

- » At the end of the visit, do you communicate your gratitude to the client for their business?

- » At the end of the visit, do you suggest an appointment for rebooking?

- » Are clients aware of your incentive referrals, package or family discounts, special discount or happy hour pricing, current coupons or offers?

While you cannot lose sight of the quality of service which must remain your first priority during each appointment, it is the 'extra' things you do that tell the client you are personally interested in their well being. It is the attention that you pay to creating an ideal client experience that will set you apart from the competition, ensuring that clients feel that you value their business (rather than take it for granted).

simply essential

You have heard it before, and it's true. Your clients will notice when you take the time to do something personal for them. A personal thank you note written to each client takes only minutes a day, and costs very little (e-mail thank you notes cost even less), but will go a long way toward reinforcing your role in the lives of your clients. It is a personal touch in an impersonal world. It conveys your gratitude for their patronage. It is an opportunity for you to remark on a topic of conversation or area of concern they shared with you, so that they know you truly cared and listened. It is a moment when you can ask, "Were you satisfied with your haircut (or massage, or manicure, etc.), do you have any questions about care or maintenance, and is there anything else that I can do for you?"

It is another opportunity for you to ask them to book their next appointment or to ask for a referral. It is a simple act, but very few people take the time to do it. If you make this activity part of your professional routine, it will get noticed, it will bring clients back. It will facilitate more referrals. It will provide you with more opportunities to communicate with your clients.

Order salon-branded thank you notes that you can personalize with a message and signature. Include a copy of your business card (every time) because it is the perfect way for your client to refer a friend or family member to you. If space allows, place a menu, client referral or special offer on the inside flap or back of the thank you note. If you have a points system, you can customize the note by including any points the client has accumulated as well as how many additional referrals, purchases, service visits, etc., that they need to move to the next rewards level.

simple rewards

Due to the recession of the last decade, more people than ever have returned to using coupons out of necessity and out of desire. Reward repeat clients with a periodic discount or free add-on service when they rebook, or after they have completed a certain number of appointments, purchased a certain level of retail products, or referred a friend to your business. Give service and retail coupons to clients and prospects via personal thank you notes, newsletters and e-mails and make them available on your web site.

simple steps

You may be able to increase service and/or retail sales through a simple rewards program where incentives are awarded in direct proportion to client expenditures, either in gross dollars or dollars spent on non-basic services or retail products, or both. The more a client spends in a given time period, the greater their reward. Or keep it simple and offer a frequency-based punch-card style reward or package discount.

simple recognition

Recognition is... free! Have you considered a 'client of the week' (or month) feature in-salon and in your newsletter? Recognize clients for work in the community or other achievements. Draw attention to worthy causes they support. Herald (with permission and with respect to privacy) the arrival of new babies, new spouses, promotions, retirements, etc. Select a deserving 'client of the month' to receive a free service or makeover. Ask clients to nominate a deserving member of the community who deserves a makeover or free service (or series of services). Document recognition in your salon through press releases to your local newspaper and periodicals.

simple appreciation

Implement a (formal) thank you note program for all clients with the goal of thanking 100% of your clients. Try it for a month and see how easy and effective it is! Order personalized or salon-branded thank you notes and envelopes or postcards, or use e-mail. Enhance VIP client thank yous with special coupons and incentives for new client referrals. At a minimum, obtain client e-mail addresses and send an electronic thank you, or place a note of thanks on their Facebook page.

wine and chocolate wednesdays

Hold a Wine and Chocolate event on a Wednesday for VIP clients (or any interested clients) or tailor this as an appreciation event for groups of caregivers (such as senior care attendants, hospital staff, physical and massage therapists, etc.) or people in other stressful professions (teachers, fire and police force, etc.), who deserve to receive some personal care and pampering. If state and local regulations allow, incorporate the regular offer of a glass of wine into all of your Wednesday appointments or as a thank you for VIP clients at their appointments. Or create a charitable fund raiser with cover charge and proceeds after costs going to charity.

de-stress 1

In moderation, dark chocolate and red wine can have beneficial effects including endorphin release, consumption of anti-oxidants and improved attitude through indulgence. In the spirit of health, create a one time or on-going Wine and Chocolate Wednesday reception or Happy Hour as a client thank-you event. Or, reward some of your best clients with wine and chocolates to take home.

de-stress 2

Aromatherapy-based products play a role in every area of the salon and spa from ambience to services and retail products. When a client says, "that smells wonderful!" are you prepared with product knowledge to tell them why it smells so delectable and what the benefit is to their spirit? Educate clients on the aroma-therapeutic aspects of the products that you use on their hair, scalp and skin.

Enhance retail sales by offering aromatherapy gifts for moms, teachers, coaches, friends, family and others, or by using them as client thank you gifts.

In April, display aromatherapy-based products along with fact sheets about the additional benefits provided through the design of the fragrance. Incentivize retail or service purchases with aromatherapy-based products or miniatures/samples as free gifts-with-purchase. Thank your most valuable clients with miniature sizes of aromatherapy-based products. Take entries and hold a drawing at the end of April for a free product or basket of products. In all cases, include product knowledge for clients about the aromatherapy benefits of products in order to promote current and repeat retail sales, and collect client data for addition to your client and prospect database for communications.

de-stress 3

If you offer (or are qualified to administer) scalp, neck, or hand massages, consider offering these services, or miniature versions of them as free customer-appreciation add-ons in April. Alternately, or if these are already part of your service menu, offer them at a reduced price, with related retail as a discounted package, or as a thank you for rebooking. The extra 5 to 15 minutes you spend with the client will go a long way to solidifying your role as their stylist and salon of choice. Where else could they receive such personalized extra attention?

de-stress 4

Hold a 'de-stress the client' contest or drawing where clients enter themselves and a friend and winners receive (for instance) $25 gift certificates for use in May. Or tailor this as a perfect gift for Mother's Day with the winning entry receiving a gift certificate for themselves and their mom or daughter for use in May. Follow up! All entrants should receive a special related offer from you via e-mail or mail.

prom

Spring means formals, up-dos, nights on the town, and the constant need to look 'simply smashing, dahling!' Help de-stress parents who have children in high school by creating Prom preparation packages. Suggest to parents and students that they pre-book end-of-school-year event and graduation appointments at the same time. These are great events to extend group rates for multiple bookings or groups of friends, and another opportunity for you to partner with formal wear, florist, restaurant, or limo services to cross promote or create larger, one-stop-shopping packages for clients.

simple math

Pre-sell packages of 6 haircuts at $6 off to be used in 36 weeks (for women) or 6 haircuts at $3 off each, use within 18 weeks (for men). This brings female clients back to the salon every 6 weeks or male clients every 3 weeks at a time when finances might be causing them to extend the time between visits by an extra week or more. In addition, receiving a break on the price of the cut may make clients more likely to purchase additional retail products with the money they saved. You can also use a $6 off 6 package to soften the introduction of a price increase, or as a suggestion for a great Mother's Day Gift!

April Observances and Charitable Causes

April is National Stress Awareness Month; focus promotion themes on stress causes, relievers and remedies, like diet, exercise, aromatherapy, music, massage – the possibilities are endless! Partner with dieticians, fitness trainers, yoga instructors, and massage therapists to craft education and offers for clients.

Set up point of purchase aromatherapy products with signage clearly pointing out benefits. This is a great opportunity to find a local candle maker, wine shop or chocolatier for cross marketing (exchange coupons and samples to give to one another's clients) or for cooperative marketing packages. You can even provide another point of retail for these businesses either on a commission basis, or purchase items at wholesale in order to expand your own retail offerings with these items that will make great gifts year-round.

Some of the people in our communities who carry the most stress are those who carry the weight of providing care for others in addition to themselves. Child care providers, senior care providers, health care providers, teachers, people caring for aging parents, disabled children, etc.

Make a personal difference by asking clients for nominations and awarding people in your community special De-Stress makeover, massage (or other services) awards. What a great surprise it would be for a deserving someone in your community to receive an unsolicited reward; it could result in new clients and it provides great word of mouth buzz (and fodder for your next press release) for your business.

April Planning and Tasks

Select from manufacturers promotional offerings in light of what you have planned for May and June promotions and events.

Purchase any last minute items needed for Mother's Day, design and print (or order) special gift certificates and products for Father's Day, summer skin care and summer impulse-buy products (sunscreen, hand sanitizer, lip balm, etc.), items for your May bridal show, and items needed for wedding, anniversary, bridal or graduation packages. Identify and order any special gift certificates, postcards, flyers, and supplies still needed for events or promotions coming within the next 6-8 weeks (all the way into July).

Set aside and take the time to plan ahead. You should be completely finished with preparations to support Mother's Day and May events early in April. Complete planning for Father's Day, wedding and graduation promotions, and plan events to celebrate the end of school year and beginning of summer.

Communicate in April

Items to include in your email or print newsletter, web site and direct mail communications this month:

- » April-May events, promotions, charitable activities and contests
- » Prom, graduation and other end-of-school year events
- » Information about aromatherapy benefits of products you sell
- » Highlight stress-relieving services or products
- » Mother's Day (and even begin talking about Father's Day)
- » Promote your May Bridal Show and your bridal hair, skin and makeup packages
- » Last chance for retail or service promotions expiring in April
- » Last minute openings on the books
- » March winners, April contests, drawings and opportunities

April Calendar / Suggested Communications and Tasks Schedule

SUN	MON	TUE	WED	THU	FRI	SAT
1st week of Month						
1st of April - Merchandise for April 1st of April – Begin collecting entries for April contests						
		Order signage, event supplies and promotional materials for May promotions			Send April Newsletter with coupons, announce contests and winners, new products and services, coming events, openings still on the books, events and promotions	
2nd week of Month						
		Order in gifts, salon-branded items, impulse buy and other items for May			Write press releases for any events/results reporting or future events / charitable focus	
3rd week of Month						
		Layout plans for June promotions			Send April "last chance" promotions and openings on the books e-mail and/or direct mail	
4th week of Month						
Last day of April – Take down any April-only promotions Last day of April – Draw April contest winners						
	Begin marketing Father's Day and June promotions	Order event supplies, postcards, gifts and salon-branded items needed for June promotions			Send May focus e-mail / direct mail	

April Worksheets

$_____ Retail Sales Goal

Promotions_____

_____

_____

_____

_____

$_____ Avg. Retail/Client

$_____ Retail Sales Results

$_____ Service Sales Goal

Promotions_____

_____

_____

_____

_____

$_____ Avg. Service/Client

$_____ Service Sales Results

$_____ Event Revenues Goal

Events _____

_____

_____

_____

_____

#_____ Attending Event/s

#_____ Apts/Booked at Event

$_____ Event/s Sales

$_____ Total Event/s Results

$_____ Charity/Fund Raising Goal

Charity Events _____

_____

_____

_____

_____

#_____ Attending Event/s

#_____ Apts/Booked at Event

$_____ Charity Event/s Sales

$_____ Total Charity Results

April Marketing Summary

Marketing Partners: _____

_____

_____

_____

Marketing Collateral Needed (or Used): _____

_____

_____

Other Efforts:

#_____ Number of Clients New to Salon

%_____ Client Retention Rate (90 days)

Retention Efforts: _____

_____

or % _____ Clients Rebooked at Appointment

$_____ Gift Certificate Sales

#_____ Contacts added to marketing / e-mail database

May

accidental marketing

In mid-2009 I had a series of conversations with different small business owners to brainstorm quick, fun and easy events they could hold to bring in new clients, groups of girlfriends, or generate more 'bring a friend' business.

As we discussed marketing messages, e-mail and direct marketing, and ways to craft offers, I found myself saying over and over again, do x, y, or z and "just by accident" you are bound to attract new clients or sell more retail.

I was starting to feel a little embarrassed at the lack of strategy reflected in the statement until one of the salon owners clued me in to the fact that the majority of professionals in the salon and spa industry are, in fact, marketing by accident.

When asked about marketing, the vast majority of stylists and other industry professionals confidently assert, "I'm already doing marketing." When asked what your marketing consists of, the reply is that you are doing "word of mouth marketing." When pressed for definition, your response reveals, essentially, that you feel you are such an incredible stylist or create such an amazing experience for your clients that they simply cannot wait to get out of the chair and go and tell everyone they know about how wonderful you are. This is not word of mouth marketing, this is accidental marketing.

this is not word of mouth marketing,
this is accidental marketing

To give you an idea of how effective it is as a business strategy, let me ask, would you do accidental bookkeeping, hoping that clients remember to pay you, and pay you the right amount, without giving them the bill? Accidental accounting? Tax reporting? Accidental haircuts or color?

There are many tasks relative to running your business that you approach intentionally and perform with purposeful, step-by-step methodology every day. You know that these tasks are mandatory and that you need to follow a certain formula in order to get a certain result – and so you dedicate the time and energy required to do them. But somehow when it comes to marketing, your approach reveals that you do not view it as a legitimate, mandatory part of your business operations. In reality, marketing should receive the same level of focus and attention that all of the components of your business receive – from your professional education to your bookkeeping and billing to your technique; but it rarely does.

Are you employing the type of marketing "strategy" where you open your doors and wait for people to walk in and for the phone to ring,

are you waiting for accidental success?

wondering where all the clients are? Where you provide superior, professional, high-performing retail products that sit on the shelves collecting dust waiting for a chance to "sell themselves?" Where as a booth renter you wonder why your salon owner is not doing more to get business for you?

you are not engaging in marketing, you are hoping for accidental success

Meanwhile, those of you who *are* purposefully, actively and successfully engaged in building business know that it takes intentional action in order to produce a desired result. Accidental marketing is not a valid "word of mouth" marketing strategy. Why? In order to generate word of mouth referrals, invitations, and buzz, you have to do something that is, in fact, buzz worthy. Waiting for business to come to you accidentally might feel safer or more comfortable to you, but it is just about the least effective strategy you can employ to build your business.

111

Try at least one new thing this month designed to bring in new clients. Hold one event. Offer your clients one special promotion. Communicate with your clients proactively, on a regular basis, and make suggestions for appointment times, products and services (rather than waiting for them to contact you).

Send 'thank you' e-mails to your clients (this implies that you are collecting e-mails and building your contact database) at the end of each day, genuinely and personally thanking them for their time and their business. Let them know that you are accepting new clients, and you would be honored if they would consider referring a friend or co-worker to you.

> try something new
> every month

Create a simple reward for them for referrals (and a special offer for the individuals they refer.) Lorinda's Salon and Spa in Mill Creek, Washington, offers a simple ten dollar reward – ten for the referrer and ten for the new client – applied to the next service appointment of each. When the new client completes their first appointment, they are thanked with both a second new client thank you and an additional reward they can use on their second visit.

May Event
and Promotions Ideas

Divas. Inner Goddesses. Matriarchs. Brides. Wives. Mothers. Daughters. Sisters. May is about the incredible women in our lives, the women who make a difference whether they do it quietly without recognition or blaze away like shooting stars, lighting our landscape and lifting our spirits. May is the perfect month to honor the amazing women in your life and among your clientele, and the perfect time to help your clients honor and treat the women in their lives to something special.

become the hub of wedding activities—
hold a bridal show

Don't let the title scare you. When most people think of bridal shows they think of hundreds of vendors in large convention halls where most get lost in the sea of goods and services represented. But your clients are local and there are plenty of brides to go around. You can capture a nice, profitable chunk of the bridal market in your area simply by doing something you probably already do naturally, which is connecting people who should meet one another and recommending service providers to your clients.

Become the bridal connector by bringing related vendors together to offer packages and local resources to brides and bridal parties. By partnering and working with local limo services, tux and formal rentals, dress shops and boutiques, wine shops, florists, stationers, restaurants, bakeries, caterers, musicians, wedding planners, and facilities (that host weddings), you can ensure that you will enjoy a busy, profitable wedding season beginning in May and continuing into the summer, not to mention the potential for attracting new clients by cross-marketing with other businesses.

Plan to hold one or even two annual bridal shows (November or February might be good options for the off-season). Start small, keep it fun, and work with these business partners for other related opportunities such as prom and graduation packages, makeovers, girlfriend getaways, etc. If you cannot find a physical space to hold a show, remember that you can also link these services together on your web site with simple links and offers, or you can create a special web site with community wedding and bridal resources.

Make it a high priority to find one or two wedding planners in your area with whom you can partner. Chances are they already have a list of local business contacts who would love to be represented in your bridal show, be linked to on the internet and to work with you to create cross-marketed bridal and wedding party packages.

ideas for brides and babes—
limo lunch and dress hunt

When it comes to choosing the dresses, girls like to do it together. Partner with a local restaurant, wine shop, caterer or formal wear provider to book one or more bridal parties (the bride, bridesmaids, mothers, flower girls, etc.) for a Limo Lunch and Dress Hunt event.

With a first stop at the salon, demonstrate or give a bride and a bridesmaid a sample blowout, style and mini-makeover. Partner with a caterer to bring in lunch or appetizer samples and serve with a touch of champagne from the local wine shop. Partner with a local limo or shuttle service to pick up the whole group and take them to local dress shops, to a local florist to view flower options, and to a local bakery to sample cakes.

Top off the afternoon at a local wedding or reception hall for a wine and chocolate reception, inviting a couple of local wedding musicians or DJs and the men of the wedding party to join in.

This can be also a great photo-op for the wedding party (and an opportunity for you to bring in a photographer partner). Women and men of the wedding parties should leave pre-booked with you for their special day and with a bounce back offer for future services.

Don't forget to collect e-mail and other contact information; hold a drawing for a wedding-related service or gift package with items contributed by all business partners.

With an event this big, you can also gain new clients from among your marketing partners, so be sure that businesses partnering with you receive special offers for themselves and their staff.

shower them with beauty

It's a lot more fun for bridal or baby shower guests to be treated to mini makeovers, manicures, pedicures, massages and products than to play those tired old party games! Create a bridal or baby shower option to hold in your salon or spa. You might partner with a party or wedding planner, caterer, bakery, wine shop, florist and/or limo service. Make sure guests leave with a great goody bag and bounce back offer. Hold a prize drawing and collect contact information from all guests. Create a web page for local wedding or party planners where you and your business partners' bridal shower services and related gift ideas are listed.

cinco de mayo

May 5th is Cinco de Mayo; another great Happy Hour opportunity for the salon or spa. In celebration of the "Cinco" offer clients $5 off every $25 or $50 they spend on the 5th, or run the special for a whole week or month.

queen for a day

Have clients enter contact information for themselves plus another special woman in their lives (to build your contact base and promote your services). At the end of May, draw winners of free buy-1, get-1 (bring your mom, daughter or sister, etc.) services in June or simply draw for a free service or makeover in June. Ensure that all entrants receive a special offer.

inner divas

Bring out the inner diva in your clients with free mini-makeovers or touch ups. Offer clients 10% off skin or cosmetics products purchased at the time of service. If you do not normally carry cosmetics, in April purchase a nail lacquer, lipstick, eyeshadow or other cosmetics display or small introductory package for Mother's Day Gifts.

package it

May and June are full of service and product package opportunities. Bridal, prom, graduation, anniversary packages, and of course Mother's Day. In honor of Mother's Day and the incredible women in your clientele, let your female clients save $6 on their next service appointment if they rebook within 6 weeks or offer a buy-5, get-1 free hair cut (or similar service) package to use by the end of the year.

graduation parties

Plan a get together in-salon or at a local facility where kindergarten, elementary, junior high school, high school, community college or university graduates and their parents can gather for a celebration before the big day. Promote a graduation makeover package for parents and grads. Remind them that giving gift certificates is a great way to thank their favorite teachers. Partner with local restaurants, caterers, wine and gift shops to cross market goods and services or create special bundled packages.

makeover and a meal

Partner with a local brunch spot or bring in catering and create "Mom and Me" gift packages for clients to purchase for themselves and their mom (or daughters). Make it a breakfast, brunch, luncheon or tea and cross market with local caterers or restaurant, wine shop, tea shop, florists, gift boutiques, etc. Or, partner with a dress shop and have a fashion show!

teacher's bonus

National Teacher's Day is in May, plus with the end of the school year approaching, it's a great time to put together a real "bonus package" for teachers. A cut and color for summer with a scalp massage will earn your business an "A" for sure! Market this package by giving coupons directly to local schools, PTAs, school district offices, and ancillary services (don't forget the bus drivers!) Suggest that students give your "teacher's bonus" package as a gift to their favorite teachers.

May Observances and Charitable Causes

May is all about improving the quality of life for all the divas in our lives! May is the national month of many things relative to women, from honoring women in general, to women's health, vision and hearing, to osteoporosis awareness.

Consider partnering with local health professionals to present a seminar, information or screening event for women's health topics like osteoporosis, menopause, or other subjects that pertain especially to women. Provide clients with informational literature or lists of local resources.

There are probably organizations within your community that provide services to women and children who are victims of domestic violence or poverty. If you want to get really serious about helping women and children, volunteer your services at a local women and children's shelter and pamper these neglected, stressed women for an hour or two, or bring them to the salon to be 'Queen for a Day.' Consider a fund-raiser and donate proceeds from retail or services, or gather clothing, food or other needed items for your local shelters. Publicize your efforts and raise awareness for your cause with a press release to generate community attention.

May Planning and Tasks

Select from manufacturers promotions for products to support June-July-August retail and service promotions, contests and events. Purchase any last-minute items needed for your bridal show, bridal and graduation packages, or Father's Day. With summer starting, consider adding summer skin care and impulse buy products like personalized or salon-branded sunscreen mini's and lip balms to your retail offerings. Remember to plan now for items and marketing materials needed for events and promotions going out for 6-8 weeks (all the way into August).

Plans for Mother's Day, Graduation and Bridal should be in the bag by now, and Father's Day planning should be finished by the beginning of May. Plan for June-July-August including events to prevent a summer slowdown. Begin planning for Back-to-School events and promotional packages. Contact city or county parks and recreation offices and seek sponsorship of a city league team (see July) or team party or league coaches reception. Plan to send a sample product with an offer firmly attached that the parks and recreation office can distribute to all coaches, or which can be distributed to the coaches, athletes and parents of the team that you are sponsoring.

Communicate in May

Items to include in your print or e-mail newsletter, web site and direct mail communications this month:

- » May-June Events and Promotions
- » Mother's Day, Prom, Graduation, Father's Day, and Bridal packages, events and marketing partners
- » Last chance for promotions expiring in May
- » April winners, May contests
- » Last minute openings on the books

May Calendar / Suggested Communications and Tasks Schedule

SUN	MON	TUE	WED	THU	FRI	SAT
1st week of Month 1st of May - Merchandise for May 1st of May – Begin collecting entries for May contests						
		Order from manufacturers retail promotions for products to support June-July-August marketing plans; design related signage			Send May Newsletter with coupons, announce contests and winners, new products and services coming events, openings still on the books, events and promotions	
2nd week of Month						
		Order event supplies, postcards, collateral, gifts and salon-branded items for July–August contests			Write press releases for any events/results reporting or future events / charitable focus	
3rd week of Month						
		Layout plans for July promotions			Send May "last chance" promotions and openings on the books e-mail and/or direct mail	
4th week of Month Last day of May – Take down any May-only promotions Last day of May – Draw May contest winners						
		Order event supplies, postcards, collateral, gifts and salon-branded items for July contests			Send June focus e-mail / direct mail	

May Worksheets

$_____ Retail Sales Goal

Promotions_____

_____

_____

_____

_____

$_____ Avg. Retail/Client

$_____ Retail Sales Results

$_____ Service Sales Goal

Promotions_____

_____

_____

_____

_____

$_____ Avg. Service/Client

$_____ Service Sales Results

$_____ Event Revenues Goal

Events _____

_____

_____

_____

_____

#_____ Attending Event/s

#_____ Apts/Booked at Event

$_____ Event/s Sales

$_____ Total Event/s Results

$_____ Charity/Fund Raising
Goal

Charity Events _____

_____

_____

_____

_____

#_____ Attending Event/s

#_____ Apts/Booked at Event

$_____ Charity Event/s Sales

$_____ Total Charity Results

May Marketing Summary

Marketing Partners: _____

_____

_____

_____

Marketing Collateral Needed (or Used): _____

_____

_____

Other Efforts:

#_____ Number of Clients New to Salon

%_____ Client Retention Rate (90 days)

Retention Efforts: _____

_____

or % _____ Clients Rebooked at Appointment

$_____ Gift Certificate Sales

#_____ Contacts added to marketing / e-mail database

June

get your bounce back

10 cents, or maybe 25 cents if they include electronics. That's what one source estimates the average cost is to McDonald's for the toys they distribute with kids meals. (Incidentally, they sell them for $2.50 or more if you want just the toy and not the meal.)

And that's the point. These items, which have almost no actual value can become collectibles important enough to be purchased on their own at your local fast food joint, online, at garage sales, in antique shops, via classified ads, on e-bay— and at premium prices. In efforts to attract kids, fast food toys created rock star style demand (like with Beanie Babies) for items which would otherwise be in redemption bins at Chuckie Cheese in exchange for a minimal number of skeeball tickets.

Other companies have created successful premium-with-purchase programs over the years; supermarkets have done this with dinnerware, bakeware, silverware, and other items. In fact, several years ago I bought a set of china in a consignment shop because I loved the colors in the pattern, some pinks, grays, an olive green, and a silver rim. It was unusual compared to a lot of the stock china I saw in stores, and I like things that are unique. I have four kids and I love to throw big dinner parties, so I wanted to get more plates and serving pieces, but I had no idea how to find it since it's not available in retail outlets. I started looking online and after clicking on just a few links, I found out that my Noritake pattern had been sold through Safeway stores in the 50s and 60s as grocery store premium pieces. I purchased more plates and serving pieces on ebay and now have a large set— enough for any size get together I want to throw, and enough to divide for my girls later if they want it.

The idea is not new, but it's proven. Is there a premium-with-purchase type of item you can envision creating for your salon or spa? Add-ons and gifts-with-purchase are better than discounting because discounting can leave a customer feeling like they were getting ripped off at the regular price, or as though your products or services are not worth as much as they originally believed. Can you think of a low-cost collectible type of item to release for a limited time only or something you can build on to release as a series to bring clients back? A premium that could be used to get your clients back on track for a visit to the salon every 6 weeks? An item that could be used to expand and increase your retail sales?

You could create a series of 'Diva' or accomplished-women's quotes on t-shirts, coffee mugs, water bottles, key chains, or even cool nail files. You could purchase and release a series of aromatherapy candles and room scents one flavor and one color at a time. Or you could purchase

> make more reasons for clients to see you

wine glasses and/or wine charms and release them one at a time, one (charm) each month so collectors will return for the each release.

Ideally you would release a new item at the frequency at which you want clients to rebook. This does not have to be an extra expense; you do not have to give premium items away. Most grocery store premiums were not given away for free; the customer qualified to purchase pieces based on store purchases. For instance, qualifying to purchase a plate at a low cost for every $10 of in-store purchases. You can establish the same sort of program relative to service or retail sales, or even tie premiums to your salon or spa punch or rewards card. This way, you can recoup the cost of your promotional item (or even a little more) while still passing on a good price to the client.

Use e-mail to alert customers to new releases and last chance offers for premium items. Suggest ways that clients can use these items (as well as other retail items) as gifts for others or to pamper themselves. Or work with another independent seller and create a monthly event for premium item release where you also demonstrate mini makeovers, manicures, massages, cool blow out and styling techniques, have a wine tasting, and treat clients to an escape from the every day along with gifting the premium item.

If you have been looking for a way to spark retail sales and bring clients back more often, create more reasons for them to come to the salon or spa. Create a bigger space for your business in the lives of your clients. Meet more of their needs and fulfill more of their desires. Give them more reasons than their massage, manicure, hair color or haircut and style to come and visit your business.

A quick check on Google will give you access to a number of companies that sell branded promotional products. They have access to a wide variety of items from tchatchkis priced at pennies each to high end gifts. These professionals will be happy to work with you to create a premium or salon-branded line to enhance retail sales, to gift-with-purchase, to reward or incentivize loyalty, or with which to thank clients and staff. For more resources, visit www.12monthsofmarketing.net.

extend your brand beyond your walls

Last year I helped organize a non-profit auction and dinner event, and ordered branded 16 oz glasses, branded plastic ice buckets and inexpensive items for kids and giveaways from several companies online. Ordering branded items in place of generic items for things that you can either give away or reuse makes sense. When you place your company name smack dab in the middle of a desktop, personal, party or household item people will see and use over and over again, and use in the company of their friends and family, you extend your brand beyond the walls of your business.

June Event
and Promotions Ideas

Summer at Last! If you plan ahead, June should be a banner month bringing in all kinds of dad, grad and wedding clients, along with the continued development of marketing partnerships with other businesses that cater to your ideal client groups.

With the summer also comes a significant increase in the amount of time many people spend in the sun. This is the perfect time to promote products designed to protect the hair and skin from the sun and treatments designed to restore health to the hair, skin and scalp.

building business with charity benefits and fund raisers

Often when we think of fund raisers and charity benefits we picture big gala events attended by the elite of the society page, where donors drop thousands here and thousands there, most of which (hopefully) makes it to the charity being touted by the sponsors. While most of us do not have thousands to drop, we can still raise money and make personal as well as other donations that make a real difference in our communities.

What else you may not know is that you can raise revenues at the same time you raise funds for your charitable cause. You can attract new clients by promoting your efforts ahead of your campaign, writing press releases, and getting your clients on board to bring guests to your events, resulting in more clients and more sales.

choosing a cause

There are many worthy charities from nationally recognized organizations to small town causes unique to your area. So how do you choose? You do not have to take a poll or support the "in" charity of the week; you will make a bigger difference, experience greater satisfaction, and ultimately be more successful if you support a cause that has touched your life, a cause that you can discuss with real feeling as you ask your clients and staff to join you. When I was 22, I was widowed. My husband and the father of my two (then) toddlers died after a year long battle with melanoma cancer. I chose June to talk about using fund raisers to build business because of the increased exposure to the sun that occurs during the summer months and the known link between harmful rays and some skin cancers. If you need a cause to adopt, I will shamelessly ask you to adopt mine!

Here are a few ways to make fund raising beneficial to both the charitable cause and to your salon:

> » salon-or stylist branded products

You have probably seen colored bracelets and ribbons for sale with a portion of proceeds going to charity representing the wearer's support of a wide variety of causes in a wide variety of colors. You can purchase custom salon-branded products such as bracelets, sunscreen, ribbons, pins or other items to sell in the salon (or at your event) with a portion going to charity and a portion covering costs. When it comes to preventing skin cancer, perfect benefit products to have personalized or branded for your salon include sunscreen, lip balm with SPF, umbrellas, cover-ups, visors or hats.

> » events

There are a myriad of events you can hold to benefit a cause and build business; in addition, local papers may support your efforts in publicity before and after the fact, so make sure that writing press releases and contacting your local newspapers for publication is part of your charity endeavors from the planning phase through to a release generated after the event. Events you might consider for fund raising that may also attract potential new clients include auctions, dinners, receptions, walks or runs, participation in local street fairs, car washes, cut-a-thons; the options are endless.

» dollar don'ts and dos

One of the most obvious ways to do business and raise funds for charity at the same time is to set up a specified day (or days) when you will provide services for donations in lieu of dollars. You cannot dictate what the amount of the donation has to be, but you can make a "suggested minimum donation" and encourage participants to exceed it if they so desire!

The dollars are usually tax deductible for the donor, depending on the charity you are supporting. Check with the charitable organization for information about their 501(c)3 status and tax-deductible donation requirements. Publicize correctly and you may end up with new clients for the salon as well as more volunteers than you have time to "do".

If you have more people interested in participating than you can accommodate at your event, set up a second chance event or simply book them into your regular schedule. While running an event, provide a jar or other means of collection so that anyone can donate, whether or not they are actually participating in the event.

cut-a-thon for charity

To increase awareness for your businesses and for your charitable cause, take this opportunity to show unity and combine forces with a few other area salons or stylists and craft a true community charity cut-a-thon. Invite representatives from the charity and the media to attend.

Partner with a caterer or restaurant to provide snacks or beverages or have them available for purchase with a portion going to the charity. Hold a cut-a-thon for pledged donations plus donations raised at the event with all proceeds going to charity; your take will be the goodwill, prospective clients (remember to collect data from all attendees and send them off with a bounce back offer) and great public relations coverage. Don't be afraid to take bookings at the event; this is a chance for you to show off your skills to a group of prospective clients already in your neighborhood.

bachelorettes bash

Just like the bridal shower, but a whole lot more fun! Partner with a caterer or wine shop, local limo service and a nightspot. Your bachelorette party package should start with some hot-night-out hair and makeup makeovers, a glass of champagne and catered food with limo service standing by to take the wedding party out to dance and party the big night away!

june brides

Traditionally June is the biggest month for weddings so it should be your best month for bridal services. Gift certificates make great gifts for bridesmaids and mothers of the bride or groom, or thank you gifts for event planners or musicians for some pampering after the affair. If a bride-to-be or groom purchases a package for their attendants, consider offering a buy 4 get mom's makeover free or a similar offer, and give them a percentage off retail purchases at the time of service.

bride to be drawings

Collect entries all year (this is about contact collection and communications efforts for your bridal services and packages) for brides and bridesmaids with one lucky winner to be drawn in June to receive a wedding makeover for free and/or a basket full of related products. Enhance the number of entries with a few runner-up prizes.

Follow up with all contacts by sending marketing materials promoting your bridal party packages and services. Create an irresistibly enticing package by partnering with other businesses that serve the wedding market in order to create a really big prize package, or multiple prizes. Make versions of the prize packages you create with your marketing partners available for purchase by all sets of clients.

salon or stylist sun gear

Extend the brand of your salon beyond your walls and promote your services everywhere your clients go. Purchase branded impulse buy items for summer like sunscreen minis, lip balm, tank tops, hats, water bottles, flip-flops, towels, cover-ups, sun umbrellas, nail files and more for client purchase, gift-with-purchase, add-ons or client thank you gifts.

Make sure that you and your staff are wearing branded t-shirts and tank tops this summer. Salon-branded apparel can also be great thank-you gifts for your best clients!

daddy's do

Create Father's Day gift packages that will be meaningful to your bottom line as well as to recipients. Pre-sell a package of 8 haircuts at a discount of $3 each to be used by December 31st (or 4 haircuts to be used by October 15th). You will be creating a pattern of frequent rebooking, keeping your books full and giving a practical gift that practical men will appreciate – especially in our current economy. Increase the value of the package by adding a men's retail product duo in gift bag (which you should also have for sale at point of purchase and stylists stations).

daddy duo

Father's Day is the third Sunday in June. Gather male client contacts (your female clients can enter their dads, husbands, brothers, sons, or anyone to win) and at the end of June, draw a winner for a free daddy-daughter or father-son haircut in July. Send a men's grooming package offer (such as buy-3, get-1 free or take $3 off haircuts rebooked in 3 weeks) to all entries.

June Observances and Charitable Causes

Provide public service by educating staff and clients about skin cancer and prevention. Partner with a local health care provider or cancer care center to provide literature or posters for display along with fast facts, screening information and recommendations for preventing skin cancer. Consider setting up a seminar or free skin screening clinic for interested clients.

Educate clients about the products you sell that have hair, scalp or skin-protective qualities. Purchase and retail salon-branded sunscreen or lip balms with UVA protection, or purchase salon-branded hats, sun umbrellas or other skin-protective items; you will be able to sell these items in-salon throughout the summer and take them to the streets in July (see July's 'street fair' ideas).

To get personally involved, contact your local cancer care center and ask whether you can provide services with extra T.L.C. to their patients, patient's families or their staff. Ask what their needs are for fund raising or item donation efforts and give your clients an opportunity to contribute.

You know my personal passion in this area - what is yours? You will be most successful in supporting causes that have impacted you personally, whether your choose heart disease, cancer, or a victim's rights cause, for instance. Many of your clients will appreciate having a chance to make a difference in the lives of people right in your community; consider adopting a needy family or local shelter, animal shelter, or victim's advocacy group. Write a press release to publicize efforts and increase community awareness.

June Planning and Tasks

Purchase from manufacturers promotions for items to enhance your marketing plans for July, August, and September including July 4th, Summer, Back-to-School, and other promotions going out for the next 6-8 weeks (all the way into August).

Double check supplies and purchase any final items needed for Father's Day, Graduation or Bridal promotions.

Set aside time and lay out your marketing plan for the remainder of summer, including Back-to-School promotions. With the economy in its current state, parents among your clientele will value family packages for multiple cuts and family-sized products in advance of summer vacations and Back-to-School in August.

Remember that the back-to-school market is made up both of local students in need of cuts, styles, makeovers and retail products as well as those going away for college (who might appreciate liter sizes of their favorite products to take along, or care packages during the year).

Communicate in June

Items to include in your e-mail or print newsletter, web site and direct mail communications this month:

» June-July events and promotions

» Father's Day gift certificates, packages and products

» Graduation and bridal services

» Family vacation or reunion makeovers

» Summer skin and hair care, sun hair color protection and summer salon branded products

» Summer hair color trends and conditioning products – those locks are going to get dry!

» New products

» Last chance for promotions expiring in June

June Calendar / Suggested Communications and Tasks Schedule

SUN	MON	TUE	WED	THU	FRI	SAT
1st week of Month						
1st of June - Merchandise for June 1st of June – Begin collecting entries for June contests						
		Order signage, event supplies and promotional materials for July promotions			Send June Newsletter with coupons, announce contests and winners, new products and services coming events, openings still on the books, events and promotions	
2nd week of Month						
		Order in gifts, salon-branded items, impulse buy and other items for July-August			Write press releases for any events/results reporting or future events / charitable focus	
3rd week of Month						
		Layout plans for August promotions			Send June "last chance" promotions and openings on the books e-mail and/or direct mail	
4th week of Month						
Last day of June – Take down any June-only promotions Last day of June – Draw June contest winners						
		Order event supplies, postcards, gifts and salon-branded items needed for August promotions			Send July focus e-mail / direct mail	

June Worksheets

$_____ Retail Sales Goal

Promotions_____

_____

_____

_____

_____

$_____ Avg. Retail/Client

$_____ Retail Sales Results

$_____ Service Sales Goal

Promotions_____

_____

_____

_____

_____

$_____ Avg. Service/Client

$_____ Service Sales Results

$_____ Event Revenues Goal

Events _____

_____

_____

_____

_____

#_____ Attending Event/s

#_____ Apts/Booked at Event

$_____ Event/s Sales

$_____ Total Event/s Results

$_____ Charity/Fund Raising Goal

Charity Events _____

_____

_____

_____

_____

#_____ Attending Event/s

#_____ Apts/Booked at Event

$_____ Charity Event/s Sales

$_____ Total Charity Results

June Marketing Summary

Marketing Partners: _____

_____

_____

_____

Marketing Collateral Needed (or Used): _____

_____

_____

Other Efforts:

#_____ Number of Clients New to Salon

%_____ Client Retention Rate (90 days)

Retention Efforts: _____

_____

or % _____ Clients Rebooked at Appointment

$_____ Gift Certificate Sales

#_____ Contacts added to marketing / e-mail database

July

add-on marketing

There is a passage from Margaret Mitchell's American classic novel, <u>Gone with the Wind</u>, that has stuck with me for nearly three decades. Scarlet, desperate for money to pay exorbitant taxes in the post-civil war south turns to her brother-in-law, Ashley, for advice. Ashley, however, is an individual more made for reading books than practical advice and true to character, he offers Scarlet advice in the abstract that she does not understand at the time. As they stand in her dilapidated barnyard evaluating the bleak landscape, Ashley makes reference to an ancient German poem about "the destruction of the gods," highlighting the reality that there is as much opportunity and money to be made in the destruction of a civilization as in the building of one, and that the opportunity occurs much more quickly.

With the destruction of old consumer habits that accompanied the recession, some simply hunkered down waiting for the storm to pass, hoping to hold on. But others saw opportunity and decided to take control of those things within their power to create new business, retain clients, generate loyalty and grow.

In that spirit of creativity, here are 10 things you could add to your menu for clients at little or no cost, with the added bonus of creating on-going partnerships with other businesses, sharing and growing prospect lists, and sharing the costs associated with cooperative marketing and events:

1. Cosmetics Classes: Partner with a cosmetics or skin care esthetician (you may be able to 'share' someone with another salon or spa in your area) to hold cosmetics courses for employees so that you can expand both retail and services in the salon. Employees should be trained to do mini-consultations, touch ups following hair services, and in basic product knowledge for choosing the right shades and products for clients. Or, create cosmetics application classes for clients to be held in-salon or in-spa tailored to looks for teens, party-goers, weddings and special occasions, etc.

> fill slow hours with new activities

2. Fitness: Many exercise instructors work independently, renting space from local gyms or YMCA facilities. You may even have fitness instructors within your current clientele. When your hours are slowest during the week, instead of closing early, create or invite a fitness class to meet right in your salon or spa and partner with a fitness instructor (yoga, jazzercise, aerobics, dance, or martial arts) to provide instruction. Create additional offers to be cooperatively marketed to your clientele as well as theirs.

3. Cooking and Food: In the slow, post-recession economy, there are caterers, dinner preparation businesses, and dietary-fitness professionals who would welcome an opportunity to partner with you to provide literature, signage, and even classes to your clients.   Create a party-menu cooking class for appetizers or mixed drinks, or whole dinners, a 30-day meal planning class, or classes designed to instruct clients on anti-aging or other specialty diets. To create a bigger offer or program over time, work together with dietary/food and fitness experts to create multi-level packages or a series of classes.

4. Color: Home Depot made a science over the last few years of instructing women in how they can "do it yourself." You can create classes around color, partnering with home décor, home painting and repair, cosmetics estheticians and other color experts to create color consultations for your clients from hair, makeup and nails to home décor, renovation and more. Explore the science and meanings of color, how colors affect our moods, and how to combine colors to create homogenous palettes.

5. Inside and Out: Partner with a local nursery or gardening professional to create classes to instruct clients on use of color and indigenous foliage in the yard and how to create yardscapes they can be proud of. You can also teach clients about basic lawn and garden care and create "inside and out" people and landscaping packages to offer to both sets of clients.

6. Tablescapes and Party Planning: Many clients would love to throw a fantastic wedding, anniversary, graduation, or even just a great dinner party, but cannot afford professional planning help. Work with a local party planner, florist, or wedding or reception facility professional to create classes for your clients in designing their own tablescapes for entertaining and creating great party experiences for their guests. Party planners likely have extensive contact lists in your area for direct and e-mail marketing campaigns. Work together to construct party preparation package offers for both sets of clients.

7. Make Me Feel Better! Partner with estheticians or massage therapists to create classes for clients on the benefits of massage and even teach them how to give a mini hand or shoulder massage to their special someone. Create packages where clients save when they book services with your business partners. Partner with a local chiropractor and create classes for clients on the benefits of chiropractic services. Set up a meet and greet for clients in the salon where the chiropractor can perform mini-services or assessments and book appointments. Create packages to be marketed to both sets of clients.

8. Make Me Look Better! The practices of many cosmetic medical and dental service providers are hurting in today's economy where consumer spending on non-essential services is at a minimum. For them, partnering with an essential service provider like a salon makes perfect sense. Create classes in your salon for cosmetic medical and dental service providers to provide clients with tips, tricks, diet and other natural things they can do to promote healthy lifestyles and counter the signs of aging, or services that they can purchase to restore what time, weight, childbearing, and other life events have altered. Create packages that can be marketed to both sets of clients.

9. Lighten Up! Most dentists offer teeth whitening or color restoration services, and many have the ability to provide whitening services in a mobile setting. Provide education, create classes and book appointments where clients can come to have their color and teeth brightened at the same time.

10. Sweet Nothings: Who would not want to partner with caterers, candy makers, wine shops and chocolatiers to bring sweets in to the salon for retail sale or for orders for parties, work events, birthday and new baby gifts, and so much more? Create offers that are marketed to both sets of clients. Create classes for candy making and chocolate decorating where business partners teach clients how to create beautiful and irresistible desserts for their own parties and events.

Reach out to other businesses and share contacts and cross-referrals. Find at least 5 other businesses who would be willing to display your business cards or menus

> tap deep pools of clients

near their cash register or in waiting rooms (or even public rest rooms). Doctors, dentists and orthodontists share your desired demographics to some extent, as do fitness centers, exercise and dance studios. To build male clientele, get into the waiting rooms of your local car repair, oil and tire change businesses, or connect with local sports bars, sports facilities or sportsmen's organizations. As you watch new coffee, wine and gift shops opening their doors near you, be among the first to contact them with an offer to do cross-marketing. New business owners are full of energy and enthusiasm, have lots of ideas about marketing and events, and would love to build business with you – it's their number one priority!

'Add-On Marketing' is more than sharing counter space. It is reaching out in new ways to bring in new clients. Target large employers in your area and ask for permission to leave collateral for their employee bulletin boards or break room areas. Create an offer for the employees of your city offices, fire and police forces, local churches, charity organizations, health care centers. Target local schools, PTAs, and school districts with offers for teachers, administrative and other staff. While public schools may have regulations or policies which prohibit you from extending offers to their employees or students, remember that private schools are also an option.

July Event
and Promotion Ideas

July brings summer vacations, family reunions, baseball, apple pie and fireworks. The common theme running throughout the month may very well be get-togethers focused on the foods we love to eat the most - hot dogs - ice cream - corn on the cob - potato chips - soda - cake - we might as well just go with it! Focus July marketing on events that can heat things up in your business while clients cool off. Spend July preparing for a healthy Back-to-School season and start thinking about plans for the holidays (no, really!) which will need to be firmed up just on the heels of summer.

use food to do hair

You have already read numerous suggestions for food and beverage-based events, so hopefully you are well on your way to building out a regular series of social events centered around food and drink client-indulgent promotions.

Summer hours can be hit and miss with client vacation schedules but there are some things you can do to heat things up in the salon while you cool everyone off this summer. Key to some of these events is getting involved with your local parks and recreation associations to promote services and events to local city sports leagues and activities.

Find out how you can sponsor a city league team and get your business name on the backs of dozens of little baseball stars. Attend your team's games bringing coupons for services or even small branded give-aways for sports moms like branded nail files or ice-cold (filled) water bottles.

Invite your sponsored team back to the salon or partner with a local restaurant to host ice cream or snow cone socials (and sangria for the grown ups), or have a good old fashioned tailgating party at the park (first check with local regulations regarding what you can and cannot bring to public parks).

Don't be shy, take bookings; chances are the kids need cuts (and so do their moms and dads!) Begin to fill your books with back-to-school appointments now.

give it a sporting chance

Sponsor a city league team; if you don't have a child in summer sports, chances are that one of your staff or clients will. Supporting local youth sports and social organizations will help you build goodwill as well as exposure in your community. If your local parks and recreation or little league sports leagues publish seasonal programs, find out about sponsorship or advertising opportunities.

Place an ad in your local paper in support of your team and include a special offer for all city or little league team players or their parents redeemable by a code word you include in the ad.

league rules

Take full advantage of city youth activity and little league crowds. Gather contact information at the ballpark as well as in the salon for parents of city leaguers or the players themselves. At the end of July draw a winner for a free Back-to-School cut and style for one (or a few) lucky winner/s and send marketing materials with your Back-to-School or city league athlete offerings to all entrants.

coach's corner

Most youth sports league coaches are unpaid and under-appreciated, so create an offer to extend to league players on behalf of their coaches. For instance, when a league player or parent purchases $25 in retail products, let them purchase a gift certificate at half price for a haircut and style to give to their coach as a thank you from the player. Extend a special offer or give $10 off certificates to all league coaches through your city league or other parks and recreation youth sports leagues, or place an ad in the local newspaper with a special sports league player or coach code word for redemption.

snow cones and sangria

Snow cones and sangria – what a great way to cool clients off this summer! Create receptions in the salon or at a local restaurant pre-game or sponsor post-game get-togethers. Keep the menu simple with snow cones for the kids and sangria for the grown ups, along with a bounce back offer for your salon or spa. If parks or city ordinances allow you to do so, sell (or distribute) salon-branded ice-cold water bottles. If you can afford to give them away for donations you can also increase support for your favorite charitable cause!

ice cream senior social

Seniors need to beat the heat, too. Contact a local retirement community or senior center and set up ice cream socials for seniors in the salon or take the treats to them. Work in a wash and set or color and set – for the senior set; they might enjoy the sangria, too!)

reunion & vacation makeovers

We all want to look our best for those family, business, high school or college reunions when we will be seeing old friends, loved ones or in-laws who only get to see us once in a while; after all, their opinions always did matter as much as our own. Offer clients a reunion or vacation cut and color makeover at a $10 or 10% discount, with another $10 or 10% discount on their next service if they send you a postcard from their vacation destination.

celebrate independence... from bad hair

Being outdoors in the summer to hike, swim, and sport is no excuse for bad hair – banish the pony tail! Create a summer hair package that includes sun-friendly color highlights, products to extend hair color and vibrancy, a low maintenance cut, and hair care products designed to add moisture, repair and protect hair from thermal and environmental damage.

workaholics

July 5th is National Work-a-Holics Day and all of us 'workaholics' are begging you to create a workaholics hair care package to sell all year that includes $4 off 4 presold haircuts with a mini scalp or hand massage plus a hard working hair care retail duo. On behalf of all workaholics, I promise you we will try to use this up by the end of the year... get us in your books, we need your help!

fare for street fair

Many cities hold some kind of annual street fair in the summer. If yours does, take a booth. If you cannot do it on your own, partner with other stylists, massage therapists, estheticians or other independent sellers.

Don't simply hand out flyers or sell retail, take advantage of this moment to impress potential clients. Be bold! Set up a mobile station with styling products and tools, skin care products and cosmetics and either schedule models or solicit volunteers to show off your blow-dry and style, makeup application, manicure, massage or other skills right on main street. This is also a great place to sell retail products and educate the public on the benefits that differentiate professional hair color, treatments and retail products.

Get your brand out on the street, too. Wear and sell salon or stylist-branded tanks, shirts, sunscreen, water bottles and lip balm; if the sun is out, you'll sell through it all!

hot dog days

National Hot Dog Day is observed in July. Make a hot-dog-week of it and offer free hot dogs to your clients all week either during lunch or at all appointments. Create flyers to publicize your 'Hot Dog Days' and take them to local businesses, asking that they post them on company bulletin boards or place them in break areas. Include your offer and your phone number for booking appointments and suggest that they make a 'lunch' of their haircut appointment in order to save more of their free time for fun.

Hold or sponsor a hot dog eating contest at a local bar or restaurant. Donate proceeds to benefit 'hot dogs' down at the local animal shelter, or create an event designed to promote the adoption of 'hot dogs' from the shelter.

Find out who the culinary 'hot dogs' are among your clientele. Hold a recipe or cooking contest where one of the main ingredients must be hot dogs and award prizes to the best (or to all) entrants. As always, collect contact information and provide bounce back offers as well as linking them in to future communications.

Partner with a dietary expert, caterer or food preparation business to create classes to educate clients in "Cooking Beyond the Hot Dog" for their families or summer parties.

July Observances and Charitable Causes

Since the summer is all about fun for kids, focus an awareness campaign on kids who might not be having as much fun due to childhood illnesses. Create signage for the salon to promote client awareness and draw attention to local children's charities. Or get personally involved and donate time at a local children's hospital by donating services to patients in the hospital or by giving certificates to patients, family members or caregivers.

Nearly every metropolitan area has a children's hospital and most of them have adjacent housing (like a Ronald McDonald's House) where family members of seriously ill patients come to stay. If you are close enough to donate services to these family members, please do! If distance is an issue, do a fund raiser, donate funds or products to a chosen facility, or partner with a salon near them to support provision of gift certificates for patient's family members and caregivers. Write a press release to capture more attention within the community.

Create a special "Care for Caregivers" offer for the employees of your local hospitals, physician's offices, cosmetic surgeons, dentists, and senior health care or retirement centers. Contact administrative staff and ask permission to have copies placed in employee break or lunch areas or posted on bulletin boards. Make it August-only or continue throughout the year by creating receptions, happy hours and other events for this deserving crowd!

July Planning and Tasks

Select from manufacturer promotions for products to support your marketing plans for August, September, and October. Obtain any additional supplies or products needed for your Back-to-School campaign. Set time aside and layout your marketing plan and collateral needs for events going out 6-8 weeks, all the way into September. Begin thinking about holiday!

Your Back-to-School campaigns and promotions should begin in July. Multi-kid-cut discounts will be a big help for mom, but don't forget to reach out to teachers and your local PTAs— they need great hair, too! Begin planning the promotions you will run in early fall and start thinking through the initiatives and events you want to hold to meet your holiday sales goals. Plan now in order to hold a large-scale holiday retail event in early to mid-November with marketing partners in order to capture holiday spending before the mall and online retailers get all the attention.

Communicate in July

Items to include in your e-mail or print newsletter, e-mail, web site and direct mail communications this month:

- » July and August events and promotions
- » Summer socials
- » Sports sponsorships and team results
- » Tailgating parties
- » Snow cones and sangria
- » Educate clients on summer hair care and skin care
- » Last minute openings on the books
- » Last chance for promotions expiring in July

July Calendar / Suggested Communications and Tasks Schedule

SUN	MON	TUE	WED	THU	FRI	SAT
1st week of Month 1st of July - Merchandise for July 1st of July – Begin collecting entries for July contests						
		Order from manufacturers retail promotions for products to support August-September-October marketing plans; design related signage			Send July Newsletter with coupons, announce contests and winners, new products and services coming events, openings still on the books, events and promotions	
2nd week of Month						
		Order event supplies, postcards, collateral, gifts and salon-branded items for August-September contests. Focus on summer hair and skin care (repair) products			Write press releases for any events/results reporting or future events / charitable focus	
3rd week of Month						
		Begin marketing Back to School promotions and packages. Layout plans for September promotions			Send July "last chance" promotions and openings on the books e-mail and/or direct mail	
4th week of Month Last day of July – Take down any July-only promotions Last day of July – Draw July contest winners						
		Order event supplies, postcards, gifts and salon-branded items needed for September promotions			Send August focus e-mail / direct mail	

July Worksheets

$_____ Retail Sales Goal

Promotions_____

_____

_____

_____

_____

$_____ Avg. Retail/Client

$_____ Retail Sales Results

$_____ Service Sales Goal

Promotions_____

_____

_____

_____

_____

$_____ Avg. Service/Client

$_____ Service Sales Results

$_____ Event Revenues Goal

Events _____

_____

_____

_____

_____

#_____ Attending Event/s

#_____ Apts/Booked at Event

$_____ Event/s Sales

$_____ Total Event/s Results

$_____ Charity/Fund Raising
Goal

Charity Events _____

_____

_____

_____

_____

#_____ Attending Event/s

#_____ Apts/Booked at Event

$_____ Charity Event/s Sales

$_____ Total Charity Results

July Marketing Summary

Marketing Partners: _____

_____

_____

_____

Marketing Collateral Needed (or Used): _____

_____

_____

Other Efforts:

#_____ Number of Clients New to Salon

%_____ Client Retention Rate (90 days)

Retention Efforts: _____

_____

or % _____ Clients Rebooked at Appointment

$_____ Gift Certificate Sales

#_____ Contacts added to marketing / e-mail database

August

diversion-proof marketing

In the beauty industry you simply cannot use the "D" word (diversion) without evoking some kind of emotion; from a defeated, resigned shrug – to steely resolve – to passionate, crusading resistance. No matter your reaction, pretending that diversion does not impact your business and ignoring the consequences does not negate them.

As a salon professional you may feel as though the reality of diversion is out of your hands; after all, what can you do to stem the tide when big players release 'professional' products into mainstream retail outlets from the drug store down the street to the big box outlet – not to mention on the internet?

Consumers have never had access to such a wide variety of salon retail product choices available from such a large number and variety of purchasing points. From inexpensive mass-produced brands to products previously available only in the most exclusive salons and spas, if your client can "Google it", they can get it!

The good news is that you can do more than work around the reality of diverted professional products. There are actions you can take to make your business diversion-proof, ensuring that clients will come to you for products as well as services.

Marketing is much more than the ads you place or the promotions you run. Marketing encompasses every message that you send to clients, from the ones you intend to send through overt messaging to the ones you may not even be aware you are sending – the atmosphere in your salon, the attitude clients sense from your staff, the products they see on the backbar, and more. When it comes to retail products in the salon, there is often a huge, gaping hole where your messaging should be!

Do you carry products in the salon that are *truly* available to the consumer only in licensed salons and spas, or do you carry products that you know are available in your client's grocery or drugstore?   If you knowingly carry products available at local retail stores, you need to put a strategy in place through promotions, add-on services, etc., to incentivize clients to purchase from you, rather than a retail competitor. You may need to do reconnaissance at local stores to see which of your products are available there and where they are priced, and you may need to make changes to your own retail strategies accordingly.

With the purchasing power that large chains have, you cannot compete on price. So how do you give yourself an edge?

One of the most obvious answers is to carry products whose manufacturers have elected to sell exclusively through professional distribution and to the end consumer only by way of licensed salons and spas. But this is only the first step; you also have to communicate the unique benefits these products have to your clients. You must identify legitimate client needs, problems and conditions, and then you have to convince

> give yourself
> an edge

clients that the products that you carry meet their needs and solve their problems better, faster, more efficiently and more luxuriously than do those they can purchase elsewhere.

To create true exclusivity for your clients, you may elect to carry your own salon-branded line of products. This may be simpler than you think. You do not need a degree in chemistry or your own lab to have a private line. Advances in technology have made print-on-demand and other short run labeling options more possible and more affordable. This may be the perfect time to contact manufacturers with questions about creating a private label line of hair, skin, cosmetics, waxing or other products for your salon. This can work especially well for salons with a boutique feel whose client base is especially attracted by the idea of exclusivity, personalized attention and the idea that they have access to items that are not available to the general public.   Remember, it is not just by having exclusive products.   It is in the positioning, merchandising, signage, promotions, messaging – in other words, through on-going, consistent communication at multiple touch points throughout the course of your business with clients that you establish these perceptions.

Apply the same principles of marketing messaging when it comes to services that you do for products, especially when it comes to the products that you use in your services. It is likely that some of your clients have gone to the drugstore for their hair color and other professional products as a result of the recent recession and lack-luster recovery.

When it comes to hair color, what is it about the color you carry that sets them apart from the drugstore lines? If it is only in your personal ability to apply the color, you have lost the messaging war when it comes to clients

> ### what *really* sets you apart?

who want all-over color – because they can apply all-over color themselves, and are incentivized to do so from a cost standpoint, where hair color services might run into triple digits several times a year.

When it comes to nail polish, why is the manicure or pedicure the client receives from you superior to the one they can provide for themselves at home?

You must identify, differentiate and communicate the benefits inherent to your services and service-related products – from hair color and texture lines to products you use for massage, waxing, nail or skin care services, to services provided at the backbar – in a way that persuades your clients that the products you use and the way in which you use them is superior to anything they can purchase at retail outlets or perform themselves.

August Event
and Promotion Ideas

While the heat of August often belies the fact that summer is almost over, as the month-end nears and the smell of fresh pencil shavings fills the air, make August about Back-to-School, focusing on families and teachers while making one last push to promote your summer-specific services and summer skin and hair care.

One of the ways to ensure robust back-to-school sales is to make it convenient and cost effective for families to choose you to lop off those summer locks and get kids ready to face their peers. With Homecoming, fall dances, concerts, plays and other school events just around the corner, make sure clients know about your relevant service packages.

the back-to-school season—
the family and school markets

Here in the Pacific Northwest schools take lots of breaks during the school year, so summer break does not arrive until late June which makes the break between "School's Out!" and "Back to School!" painfully short, but there it is! For marketing purposes, you have to plan in a world that runs two to three months ahead of the calendar or many opportunities to build business will come and go before you have a chance to capitalize.

Create student and teacher-focused promotions that incorporate new services into your menu. Get creative and carve out new sources of revenue. Again, think of it in terms of creating add-ons; only instead of creating add-on services, you are creating add-on strategies for your marketing plan to help you discover new clients, pool resources with other business owners, build business, and increase profitability.

Catering to teachers makes sense. Teachers appreciate value and convenience and they appreciate having style that is easy to maintain and replicate. Their time is at a premium because most of their days start early and end late, so you might consider setting aside certain time blocks for teacher's appointments, or even set up a weekly teacher's happy hour. Teachers also represent much larger communities (of other teachers, parents, etc.) Many of them have a large circle of acquaintances with the potential to be a source of referrals for you to a wide network of individuals throughout your community.

Ask your local school, school district, or PTA to place a stack of flyers with your contact information and a service menu or postcard-sized offers in break rooms. Contact local schools to ask about advertising special offers to teachers, students and parents in school newsletters. Support local athletic, music, art, theater, and other programs. Attend school events, get involved in auctions and fund raisers. If the school will allow you to, provide them with copies of a flyer or large postcard that can be inserted into student folders.

get involved get noticed get busy

The back-to-school season presents a time and opportunity-concentrated market; most students get their hair cut just before the beginning of the school year. Even kids who wear their hair long get everything freshly 'mussed', and mussed with the right products, before they head back to class to face their peers. Chances are you have clients who come to you for their services but take their kids to what they perceive is a less expensive walk-in salon. They are not saving time and they may not be saving money doing this, but their perception is that they are. While clients are in the chair this summer chatting about their kids and a new school year, ask some questions to help you build your family and school markets.

"how many kids do you have, how old are they?"

When your client is checking out, book their next appointment and offer them an opportunity to book their children's appointments at the same time with some type of "family rate" discount. When you can book multiple clients and perform multiple services over the same block of time, you know that you will be making more efficient (and more profitable) use of your time. Pass some of the efficiency on to the client in the form of special rates to incentivize them to bring more of their family members to you for services.

This could be especially important to junior and high school students where peer pressure is tough. Having a custom cut and style from you, someone personally interested in the client and the well being of their families, will ensure that at least their hair is something they will not have to be nervous about.

This is a great opportunity to create some type of BOGO offer (buy-one, get-one) where the client pays full price for their cut and color and style, but saves half on their child's haircut. For instance, if a client has 3 kids, they might receive a special offer were they would pay full price for the (most expensive) two services, and receive two services at half off, or buy-three, get-one free. At this time of year, a BOGO-style offer can make a big difference to the budget of working families with school-age children and can mean years of repeat client services for you.

"where do your kids go to school?"

Target local schools, PTAs, and school districts with offers for teachers, administrative and other staff, as well as parents and school patrons. Public schools may have regulations or policies which prohibit you from extending offers to their employees or students, but private schools are also an option. While private schools may in some cases represent smaller student bodies; their parents are more likely to be part of your prime client demographic targets in terms of home ownership, income, professional work status etc.

buzz

The bottom line for teachers and parents is that they talk to one another in the parking lot, the classroom, at meetings, sporting events, the coffee shop, and even in the grocery store aisles. They share referrals. If it's good, they ask each other, "who does your hair?" It's a market worth courting and extending special offers and events to.

test (your skills) for teachers

For a charitable event in August, consider creating a 'Teacher Test' (a test of your skills and your clients' charitable spirit). Set aside a day to do free teacher's haircuts, manicures, massages or other services in exchange for donations. Encourage participation in the form of donations from all clients. Use the proceeds to purchase school supplies for needy kids in your area. Publicize before and after with press releases for goodwill, free advertising, and to raise community awareness.

Teacher's organizations, school districts and PTAs of public and private schools can be a great source of new clients and referrals. Reach out to soccer moms and school theater moms and band moms and football moms and (well, you get it) by advertising in their publications, donating to their fund raisers and becoming a local "booster."

Plan a Back-to-School Reception. Invite teachers from local schools to your salon for a relaxing mini manicure, massage or makeover. Partnering with a local caterer, provide light snacks and beverages such as sangria or champagne to celebrate the arrival of a new academic year (and remember to celebrate with them again at the end of the year!)

PTA members are often people who actively lead and influence other people in multiple areas of their lives. Create a special offer or parents-night-out event for them, it will be well worth the referrals. If you have school-aged kids, get involved in your PTA organization and seek opportunities to provide parents with offers from your business. Encourage parents to purchase gift certificates or salon and spa retail products as thank you or holiday gifts for teachers and school employees, music instructors, coaches, etc.

kids cut

Let clients with children enter to win an August drawing and encourage them to enter friends with children in the drawing too; remember that one of the main purposes of holding contests is data collection to expand your marketing outreach. At the end of August, draw a free Kid's Cut winner where (for instance) the winning client receives a free haircut for one of their children when they book their next service. Send a special kids or family cuts promotional offer to all clients.

pay it forward

Add a feel-good element to client appointments this fall. Give clients a discount or special free add-on or sample product when they bring in school supplies to be donated to needy families or local schools for kids in need.

teacher 10

No one is busier in August than the teachers and employees of your local schools. Help them get ready to head back to the classroom by giving any school employee a 10% or $10 discount on services and retail products in August.

Suggest that clients purchase gift certificates as gifts for teachers, coaches, instructors and music teachers all year. Give clients a 10% or $10 discount or free add-on service for Gift Certificates purchased for teachers or coaches.

keep 'em smiling

The second week of August is National Smile Week. Partner with a dentist in your area in a cross-marketing promotion; display one another's business cards, promotional offers, certificates, coupons and service menus. If the dentist is willing, have them provide you with free toothbrushes or flosses (or order salon-branded toothbrushes or flosses) as a give-away, gift-with-purchase or impulse buy retail item for August. Or purchase salon-branded toothbrushes or flosses and donate them to local pre-schools, day cares, elementary schools, or other organizations to go home to families.

Cross-marketing with a dentist who is also seeking to grow their business is smart because you share the demographic target of working locals who have an interest in maintaining a good appearance and good health. Share contacts for cooperative marketing efforts with events such as an open house or special wine and chocolate event tied to advice from the dentist in providing good cleaning and mouth care following wine and chocolate consumption.

August Observances and Charitable Causes

Forgive the pun, but when it comes to creating awareness in August, "it's a no-brainer." With Back-to-School and a natural focus on children, awareness issues include childhood poverty, nutrition and education. If your salon is ready for a long term project, contact a local social services office, church or school and extend free cuts on an on-going basis to a needy family in your community. Provide literature and information to clients about how they can get involved in supporting children in your local community.

Help children in your own community and make it easier for kids who are starting a new school year with backpacks, lunch boxes, pre-paid lunch cards, and donated school supplies including notebook paper, binders, pencils, erasers. Consider giving clients a discount on service or retail when they bring in new school supplies which you will donate to local social services agencies or schools.

Publicize your efforts and results with press releases.

August Planning and Tasks

Choose from manufacturers retail promotions to support your September-October promotions and events. Purchase supplies needed for events.

Design and print (or purchase) the marketing and promotional materials you need for events and promotions occurring in the coming 6-8 weeks (all the way into October).

Purchase salon-branded and other pet products for retail or giveaways for September's pet-focused events.

While it may still feel like summer, it is already time to get a handle on planning holiday promotions and retail events with cross-marketing partners and multiple vendors in November. In some salons, the holiday season accounts for up to 25% of their annual retail sales, but you have to plan ahead and begin communicating with clients early in order to capture a healthy share of the money they plan to purchase on gifts.

Finish planning promotions and events for September and October. Plan now to hold a Holiday Shop event in November and invite independent sellers, boutiques, pet stores, wine or gift shops and other local businesses in your area to participate in a Holiday Shop in-salon or at another location so that you can capture a share of your customers' holiday shopping budgets. Partner with a caterer and wine shop for food for the event and hold by mid-November in advance of the serious holiday retail season.

Communicate in August

Items to include in your e-mail or print newsletter, web site and direct mail communications this month:

- » August and September events and promotions

- » July winners and August contests

- » Report on charitable endeavors

- » Save the date for October events and your November holiday gift sale

- » Teacher and student special offers and your charitable focus

- » Suggest which retail products are 'must-haves' as well as great values for outbound college students

- » Last chance for promotions expiring in August

- » A sneak peek at what clients can expect for the fall

- » End-of-summer hair and skin care recommendations

- » Last minute openings on the books

August Calendar / Suggested Communications and Tasks Schedule

SUN	MON	TUE	WED	THU	FRI	SAT
1st week of Month						
1st of August - Merchandise for August 1st of August – Begin collecting entries for August contests						
	Focus extra marketing efforts on schools, family cut packages, PTAs, teachers, etc.	Order signage, event supplies and promotional materials for September promotions			Send August Newsletter with coupons, announce contests and winners, new products and services coming events, openings still on the books, events and promotions	
2nd week of Month						
		Order in gifts, salon-branded items, impulse buy and other items for September-October			Write press releases for any events/results reporting or future events or charitable focus	
3rd week of Month						
		Layout plans for October promotions and begin planning your Holiday Shop for November			Send August "last chance" promotions and openings on the books e-mail and/or direct mail	
4th week of Month						
Last day of August – Take down any August-only promotions Last day of August – Draw August contest winners						
		Order event supplies, postcards, gifts and salon-branded items needed for October promotions			Send September focus e-mail / direct mail	

August Worksheets

$_____ Retail Sales Goal

Promotions_____

_____

_____

_____

_____

$_____ Avg. Retail/Client

$_____ Retail Sales Results

$_____ Service Sales Goal

Promotions_____

_____

_____

_____

_____

$_____ Avg. Service/Client

$_____ Service Sales Results

$_____ Event Revenues Goal

Events _____

_____

_____

_____

_____

#_____ Attending Event/s

#_____ Apts/Booked at Event

$_____ Event/s Sales

$_____ Total Event/s Results

$_____ Charity/Fund Raising
Goal

Charity Events _____

_____

_____

_____

_____

#_____ Attending Event/s

#_____ Apts/Booked at Event

$_____ Charity Event/s Sales

$_____ Total Charity Results

August Marketing Summary

Marketing Partners: _____

_____

_____

_____

Marketing Collateral Needed (or Used): _____

_____

_____

Other Efforts:

#_____ Number of Clients New to Salon

%_____ Client Retention Rate (90 days)

Retention Efforts: _____

_____

or % _____ Clients Rebooked at Appointment

$_____ Gift Certificate Sales

#_____ Contacts added to marketing / e-mail database

September

visibility in a sea of sameness

Most of us have heard snippets of the popular "You Might Be a Redneck…" series of one-liner jokes by Jeff Foxworthy, with such gems as "If you've been married three times, and you've always had the same in-laws, you might be a redneck." No matter where you grew up, or how polished your personal pedigree, you can probably identify someone within your circle of family or friends to whom these one-liners fall dangerously close to home.

The same principle of identification applies in the salon and spa. If you slink in late with your unwashed hair in a ponytail under a baseball cap that is half covering your make-up-free, just-out-of-bed face (daring your boss or co-workers to comment) you might "just have a job." If you forget your client's name three minutes into a consultation, if you do not bother to rebook them, if you never suggest retail products for home use, and if you would rather "eyeball" your color mixture than measure it, you might "just have a job" (and you might not have that one for long).

If all you want is a job, and all you need is a paycheck, skip the rest of this chapter lead-in, in fact, skip the rest of the book. An out-of-work friend once begged me to help them find a job – well, sort of. They actually told me, "I don't need a job, I need an income," and asked me about to help them get involved with get-rich-quick internet opportunities they perceived required nothing more than a web site set up. While a few people occasionally do "get rich quick," in most cases they do so *only after* spending years developing their craft, doing research, learning the ropes, and working hard.

I know you didn't get in to this business for the marketing part of the job. You may have had a short introduction to marketing as part of your schooling, but you were probably more interested in learning your craft, developing your techniques, and making art with hair and skin than you were about the mechanics of marketing.

> marketing yourself is
> essential in a sea of sameness.

No matter how talented you are or how well you treat your clients, there are other people who "do what you do." Marketing includes activities that you engage in with the purpose of persuading people that you "do what you do" in a way that is better artistically and better for them as a client and is a better value in general than do others in your profession. Marketing is a purposeful, scripted way to give clients reasons and opportunities to choose you.

As a new stylist you enter a professional world where your peers have already established clientele, and where there are many other choices for the potential clients in your community. As a new stylist, your most important responsibility is not what you do behind the chair; it is to build your client base. Don't get me wrong, what you do behind the chair matters very much. But you cannot "do what you do" behind the chair if no one is sitting in it!

Your co-workers may have referrals to help you get started and can be valuable resources. Ask them to tell you how they built their client bases when they first started and what activities they would recommend now for new stylists. Ask them what groups of potential clients they think you should be trying to attract (based on what they know about your skills, training, interests and personality). They may have done some really creative things in the beginning, they can tell you a lot about clients in your community and about attracting clients that will be a good fit for your salon as well as for you, as a stylist.

Go further. As a student you probably loved opportunities to create styles that were way out of the box, stretching your creative and technical skills and resulting in a look no one else could achieve – because no one else is 'you.' Your approach to building business and marketing yourself deserves the same creativity and individualization; to be successful you will have to stretch your skills and tap into your own personality and interests in order to produce results.

Take a look around at other businesses and independent sellers. They have learned that parties and events (taking their products and services outside to "where clients are") and creating social networks builds business and sales in a way that individuals who are simply waiting for people to walk in to their store, salon or spa cannot compete with.

Take Justice for Girls, a 'tween' clothing store in the mall. Yes, they sell clothes, but they are also 'scooping' business that should belong to the professional beauty industry. Their teenage staff host hair and makeup birthday

> go where
> clients are

parties for 'tween' girls in groups – all the while their moms, sisters, and other women are standing by watching, and shopping and leaving with a bounce back coupon (and reasons to return). And it's contagious; once one girl has a party there, they all want to have their next party there.

Why should they be stealing your business? Who knows more about applying makeup or nail polish, and who has better products? Who could better teach pre-teens and their moms, aunts, sisters, and other chaperones how to create a party make-up look?

Hosting birthday, girls night, prom or graduation makeover parties, or bridal or baby showers featuring styling and makeup services to girls of all ages creates opportunities for you to gain multiple clients, sell retail products, and book appointments – and all in a 2 or 3 hour space of time. You can host events in the salon, or contract to perform mobile services at party sites. There are many ways to build business when you unleash the same levels of creativity and uniqueness in your marketing that you do in your craft.

September Event
and Promotion Ideas

September is 'Healthy Aging Month,' so if you offer skin care products and services in your salon, this month presents a host of event and promotion ideas from free skin analysis and prescriptives to mini-facials, treatments, an "open bar" skin bar educational event with an esthetician (great for retail sales!) and don't forget the healthy-skin, anti-aging cosmetics.

September is a national focus month for pets and you undoubtedly have hundreds of pet owners and animal lovers in your clientele and in your greater community. Partner with local veterinarian, groomers, pet shop or boarding facilities to create co-marketed promotions and events, and buy in salon-branded or just-plain-fun pet bowls, brushes, and shampoos.

animals have hair, too!
the truth about cats and dogs

According to the Humane Society (humanesociety.org), 39% of US households own at least one dog, and 34% of US Households own at least one cat. A significant number of those households, in both cases, own more than one pet.

A few enterprising salons have already realized that they have an opportunity to expand retail sales by carrying pet shampoo and care supplies; it's a great opportunity to expand your retail in pet care and fun or salon-branded pet supplies such as food and water dishes, brushes, pet (lint) rollers, etc. Bringing this kind of one-stop convenience to the pet owners among your clientele is also a natural extension of 'what you do' in bringing quality products clients can trust to meet the needs of their pets when it comes to skin and fur care.

If you love animals yourself, post a bulletin board in the salon in September to hold pet pictures, starting it off with one of your own. Encourage clients to bring in photos of their pets or submit them to you online via your web site or e-mail in order to save a percentage or dollar amount on the retail pet products they purchase (and/or their people hair care products, too.)

This is a significant area of opportunity when it comes to networking, cooperative and cross marketing with local veterinarians, dog groomers, pet stores, breeders and kennels. You share similar demographics for 'ideal client' markets and many pet care providers have very loyal followings. Some are already even engaged in regular print and e-mail marketing. You also share values because you are all concerned for the health, well being, and appearance of your clients. Create open house events, pet receptions, off-leash park tailgating days and other opportunities for cross-promotions.

For a charitable aspect, add an event to support your local animal shelter with dollars or by encouraging (or even facilitating) pet adoptions to good families. You can offer to post pictures of local shelter animals in the salon or online, provide applications, and create a special offer for clients who adopt a shelter pet in September (and for all your pet-loving clients).

man and beast grooming package

Reach out to attract clients among area pet owners by partnering with a local groomer who has the ability to provide mobile services to come to your location and provide pet grooming while your clients receive their services. It will take cooperation and coordination ahead of time to co-book your pet-loving clients. Partner with the groomer to create a package which will be offered to their clientele as well as yours, offering a dollar or percentage off services occurring simultaneously and accompanied by a second bounce back offer if they prebook their next service appointment (within 4 weeks for men, 6 for women, and as prescribed by the groomer for pets!)

a picture's worth a thousand ... pennies

When your client brings in a picture of their pet that makes you say "awwwww..." give them Ten Paws ($10) off their service or retail purchases totaling $50 or more.

food 'n' shelter

Contact your local shelter to find out if there are items they need and accept as donations and offer clients a free add-on service or discount when they bring these items in or make a cash donation to the shelter. Create awareness for the shelter as well as your business; at the end of September, write an article about this effort as a press release for print in your local newspaper and submit it along with testimonial from the shelter as well as a picture of a four-legged shelter friend that tugs at the heart. If possible, create an on-going discount to extend to pet-lovers in conjunction with support of the shelter, and ask the shelter to provide patrons with a copy of your offer.

shelter me

Create a special offer for clients who adopt a shelter pet in September. To facilitate the opportunity for clients, partner with your local shelter to create an in-salon event to pair clients with adoptable pets on a Saturday. Publicize in advance through newspapers and community resources, don't forget to post on your supermarket or community center bulletin board.

retail opportunities

A growing number of salons are carrying professional retail items for pets including shampoo and other hair care products: toys, collars, bowls, brushes and other supplies. It's an area where you can experiment with little risk; if you don't want to buy in products yourself, partner with a local veterinarian or groomer and offer to give them shelf space in return for commission on items sold. Your clients will appreciate the convenience of not having to make a trip to the pet store. And don't forget the bling! Collars, dishes and holiday pet-wear make great impulse buys and gifts.

pet owners paradise!

If you brought in retail products for pets, give pet owners a discount on retail purchases for their pet when they purchase retail products for themselves. Or, in conjunction with a groomer, extend an on-going discount for dual pet-and-owner grooming bookings or product purchases.

pet owners patronage

Like parents with kids, pet owners have regular extra expenses – so give them a break! In another data-collection focused contest, allow clients to provide their contact information and that of their friends-who-own-pets and draw a winner at the end of September for a free hair cut in October. If working with a groomer this contest award should include a free cut for both owner and pet! Extend a special offer to all pet-owning clients after the drawing.

swap party

September 10th is "Swap Ideas Day." While ideas are great, my guess is that it might be more fun to swap jewelry, jeans, shoes, handbags, home decor or art – and more. Create a Friday-Saturday event to get people in the door for a special "Swap Party." Any boutiques, gift shops, or independent salespeople that you partner with should commit to cross-marketing this event to their customers. Plan to demo a great cut, mini massage, mini manicure or mini makeover and to sell impulse buy and retail products at the event.

you might have to act your age... but you don't have to look it!

September is Healthy Aging Month which is an ideal time to promote anti-aging hair and skin care or make-up products and services. Or partner with a local esthetician or dermatologist to provide healthy aging retail promotions, events, and education to your clients.

read all about it

September 8th is International Literacy Day and kids have just gone Back-to-School. Consider holding a book drive for a local after-school children's program, day care, school or children's services organization along with a special offer for clients who donate money or books in-salon.

planning makes perfect

October is Long Range Planning Month. Set aside at least one full day in October to review or create a systematized, measurable and trackable long range plan and set personal goals. Set aside a day or weekend to talk about the mission and goals of your business, to get employee buy in and to create a blueprint for the coming year. Put your plan on paper and give copies to a mentor or trusted friend; review progress at least quarterly in the coming year. Include your distributor sales consultants or a marketing professional for additional resources and expertise or invite other salon professionals to help you with ideas.

September Observances and Charitable Causes

September is Healthy Aging Month. Increase awareness of how aging can affect your clients health and appearance from skin and hair care to cosmetics, or even apparel. Just like Oprah, you can work with local retailers to create a 'fashion show' to demonstrate how clients can dress age-appropriately and still look their youngest-best.

One of the best ways to stay young is exercise! Partner with a local fitness expert (such as a jazzercise or yoga instructor) to cross market a promotion or services and provide literature to clients on healthy living. Partner with a local physician or dietician to provide clients with information or a seminar about how they can modify their diet in order to look and feel younger, and to be healthier.

Partner with a geriatric specialist to provide seniors with a healthy-aging seminar or series, provide information to clients about how they can better help aging parents or grandparents to look and feel their best, or what clients should be doing now to combat the effects of aging as they grow older.

This month's recommendation for your charitable focus is to support a local Animal Shelter, emergency services or animal rescue organization. You can combine a number and variety of events, promotions, client discounts or retail sales to raise awareness for the shelter, increase adoptions, and raise funds or supplies for donation.

September Planning and Tasks

Order retail products from manufacturers September-October, November-December and Holiday offerings to support your promotions for October and continuing through to the end of the holiday season. The more sales you capture in October and November for holiday, before shoppers focus on traditional retail outlets, the better. Think outside the box and try some new point of purchase and impulse buy type items for the holiday season.

Use messaging in displays, postcards, newsletters, and station talkers to speak overtly to customers about the items you are suggesting for gifts, including gift certificates themselves. Don't assume that clients know that you have products that would make great gifts for their co-workers, friends or family; make it obvious and easy for them to find them at the point of purchase. Partner with local boutiques, wine shops, coffee shops, gift shops, artisans, etc., for combined holiday-suggestive point of purchase displays and combination offers. Purchase salon-branded novelty, party, hostess and gift items.

Develop marketing and promotional materials for events, retail promotions and contests going out through December. Early planning is vital to a successful holiday season, especially since you might only see clients twice from October to December. Plan now for your complete slate of October, November and December events and promotions. Tell clients to "save the date" for the Holiday Shop event you are holding in conjunction with other vendors in early-mid November. Choose one good holiday charitable endeavor to support like adopting a family, shelter, pet shelter, or children's services, etc., that will speak to your customers emotions and help fulfill their need to give to others in the community.

Communicate in September

Items to include in your e-mail or print newsletter, e-mail, web site and direct mail communications this month:

» September and October events and promotions

» November Holiday Shop retail event 'save the date'

- » September contests and August winners

- » Extend your August back-to-school efforts by suggesting 'care package' items for college students; continue to suggest retail products and gift certificates as gifts for teachers and coaches

- » Promotions expiring in September

- » New products coming for October and holidays

- » Last minute openings on the books

September Calendar / Suggested Communications and Tasks Schedule

SUN	MON	TUE	WED	THU	FRI	SAT
1st week of Month 1st of September - Merchandise for September 1st of September – Begin collecting entries for September contests						
		Order from manufacturers retail promotions for products to support October-November-December marketing plans; design related signage			Send September Newsletter with coupons, announce contests and winners, new products and services coming events, openings still on the books, events and promotions	
2nd week of Month						
		Order event supplies, postcards, collateral, gifts and salon-branded items for October, November and December contests			Write press releases for any events/results reporting or future events / charitable focus	
3rd week of Month						
		Complete / continue to layout plans for October, November and December promotions			Send September "last chance" promotions and openings on the books e-mail and/or direct mail	
4th week of Month Last day of September – Take down any September-only promotions Last day of September – Draw September contest winners						
		Design and select salon-branded holiday wear and items for holiday retail			Send October focus e-mail / direct mail	

September Worksheets

$_____ Retail Sales Goal

Promotions_____

_____

_____

_____

_____

$_____ Avg. Retail/Client

$_____ Retail Sales Results

$_____ Service Sales Goal

Promotions_____

_____

_____

_____

_____

$_____ Avg. Service/Client

$_____ Service Sales Results

$_____ Event Revenues Goal

Events _____

_____

_____

_____

_____

#_____ Attending Event/s

#_____ Apts/Booked at Event

$_____ Event/s Sales

$_____ Total Event/s Results

$_____ Charity/Fund Raising
Goal

Charity Events _____

_____

_____

_____

_____

#_____ Attending Event/s

#_____ Apts/Booked at Event

$_____ Charity Event/s Sales

$_____ Total Charity Results

September Marketing Summary

Marketing Partners: _____

_____

_____

_____

Marketing Collateral Needed (or Used): _____

_____

_____

Other Efforts:

#_____ Number of Clients New to Salon

%_____ Client Retention Rate (90 days)

 Retention Efforts: _____

_____

or % _____ Clients Rebooked at Appointment

$_____ Gift Certificate Sales

#_____ Contacts added to marketing / e-mail database

October

loosen up tippers (in any economy)

The wait staff at my favorite restaurants must love to see me come back through the door because I am both a low-maintenance customer and an incurable over-tipper. In fact, one time when I treated my husband to dinner, he took a look at the tip I had left and said he wished I would start tipping him for mowing the lawn.

It's not that I don't know how to "double the tax" or calculate a percentage. It is out of sheer appreciation for good service, a friendly attitude, and the knowledge that people who work for tips truly need them to make their living in addition to their hourly wage. And my natural propensity for generosity is compounded by the knowledge that everyone doesn't always tip appropriately – I am entirely confident that the good karma will come back 'round to me!

In my early 20's, my husband's bread, butter and tuition depended on the tippers who entrusted their cars to the valets at an upscale hotel in Grand Rapids, Michigan. With base pay at just a couple of dollars an hour, tips were needed just to achieve minimum wage, let alone provide a livable wage. I doubt that most guests gave it much thought; but for the most part, they rewarded good attitudes and service with appropriate gratuities.

One interesting tidbit we learned about tippers is that you cannot judge a book by its cover. As a valet, sometimes you would find that the guy with the BMW would skate, while the guy with the Ford Taurus paid for dinner. With no rhyme or reason, you soon learned to give good service, provide directions and assistance and do it with a cheerful demeanor because it is who you are, rather than playing any games for tips. If you don't have good interpersonal skills and really don't care about other people, it comes through, no matter what kind of job you have (and if you do not have these skills, maybe you shouldn't be in a 'people' business!)

We all know the economy is tight; in fact, we have grown tired of hearing about it. Even writing it feels cliché. Fewer customers are coming through the door, and many others are coming back less frequently. Business is slow and tips per client are down no matter what gratuity-dependent profession you are in. And it's not about greedy or mean-spirited customers, either. As you know from daily interactions with clients, they are hurting too. You would probably prefer that your clients continue to come in to you for services even if they don't have the extra money to tip you at the end of their appointment, than to stay away.

As stylists, estheticians and therapists you may be continuing to put your heart and creativity into your work, delivering professional, caring, thoughtful service to each client who comes in the door; and while your efforts may be consistent, they may no longer be as consistently rewarded. The good news is that the same principles that work to build business, referrals, retail sales and client loyalty help to build compensation – and tips, as well.

The phrase 'exceptional customer service' has been overused to the point that it no longer carries weight. 'Exceptional customer service' is supposed to be the

what's so special about you?

norm at so many businesses that what is supposed to be 'exceptional' is now the norm – get it? The irony is that while many owners and managers confidently assert that their business provides exceptional customer service, very few actually do. Many people, when asked, state that "the difference" in their business is the people; but how can it be proved? The truth is that for better or for worse, one of the differences in *any* business is the unique blend of individuals who provide services and products to customers.

So how do you use your unique blend to really make a difference in your business?

By simple definition, what is "exceptional" is beyond the norm. If the accepted standard is meeting client expectations in a courteous, personable way, in a clean, welcoming environment, providing them with the desired results for hair, skin, nails, etc., then you have to know what it takes to exceed expectations in a way that is exceptional.

This hit home to me recently in a powerful way. My mom is considering switching dentists, and I made a recommendation. She didn't ask me if the dentist had a soft touch. She didn't ask if his staff was nice. She didn't ask about the quality of his work. She asked me if the dentist I am recommending does 'paraffin dips.'

When I asked what she meant, she told me that her current dentist dips her hands in a paraffin dip and then wraps them in plastic at the beginning of her appointment. She says she is more relaxed and stays warm all during the procedure; plus, days later, she still has baby-soft hands. At her last visit, to top things off, she was awarded the daily flower bouquet from the staff.

go beyond the norm

This, my friends, is exceptional! Can you imagine a scenario where your client recommended that their friends come to you for service, and they were asked whether you provided teeth whitening services? Or had a gift shop? Or served lunch? Or had boutique clothing or accessories for sale? Or provided other non-salon-traditional services or products?

Salons and stylists who truly want to set themselves apart simply have to go beyond the norm in order to do so. Whether it is in add-on services, samples, or the environment and "extras" available to clients within the salon itself, *something* that the client experiences as a regular part of their appointment needs to be *surprisingly more* than what is expected.

It is exceptional to provide a client with a free sample; whether it is a product sample, or a free mini add-on service. It is exceptional to give the client a quick touch up around the edges of their foundation, blush, and eye shadow after their shampoo and style. It is exceptional to provide a client with a hand-massage or brow wax while giving their hair a deep conditioning at the shampoo bowl.

Give clients more and unique reasons to visit your business. It is exceptional to schedule wine tastings, fashion shows, bridal fairs, baby or bridal showers, girls nights out, etc., in the salon for clients. It is exceptional to find partners such as party planners, the owners of local shops and restaurants, local celebrities or civic groups and the like to partner with to cross-market and hold cooperative events. It is exceptional to create and organize "buy local" campaigns within the community (particularly relevant with the holiday season closing in fast!)

And sad to say that even after all the reminders service professionals are given on this point; it is still exceptional to send a personal thank you note, client or referral reward in the mail after an appointment. (But, happy day, it is so easy to do!)

Set yourself apart. You know the value of ongoing education; but how many times do you make your clients aware of recently attended classes, the quality of the educators, the cost of the class, and how many times do you make it a point to tie that in and actually verbalize to clients that you spent this money specifically so you could bring them a new, improved result? Have you considered setting up an event immediately after receiving new technical education and inviting VIP clients in for an exclusive demonstration or your new skills and products? Do you cross train employees in new technical skills and demonstrate this through pairing while clients are in the chair?

You set yourself apart by providing samples of products and mini-services, verbalizing benefits to clients, and making it easy for them to purchase retail products or rewarding them with a specially priced full-size add-on at their next appointment. Consumers rightly view stylists as the experts on products and yet overwhelmingly indicate in industry surveys that their stylists continue to remain silent about products during appointments.

Demonstrate your expertise to clients by taking the time to understand their specific hair and skin needs, to address them honestly about these conditions, and to have the right products to recommend to them. Products not only intended to bolster retail sales, but products which honestly deliver real results that clients recognize through use at home.

Finally, as a salon owner or manager, you may need to educate clients who may be unaware of the extent to which stylists or booth renters in your salon are dependent upon gratuities over and above the cost of services. Just as some corporations provide constituents with an "annual report," you can get creative in your communications with clients to let them know where the dollars go, and ask for more referrals, client feedback, and more.

October Event
and Promotion Ideas

For women, there are moments of sorority in life. Moments of joy, fear, exultation and loss that only another woman can truly understand. To set October aside for women in the salon seems fitting – to honor those who have succumbed and those who have survived breast cancer, and to work together to raise awareness, prevention, and ultimately work toward finding a cure.

In an industry where so many aspects of business naturally revolve around women, there are few of us whose lives have not been directly impacted by breast cancer whether ourselves, a loved one, a co-worker or friend. Let's make October the month of the woman. Strong, vibrant, and healthy!

cutting cancer, building business, cutting hair

There are several organizations you can get involved with when it comes to fighting breast cancer (or other cancers), and as important as raising funds might be the difference you make in raising awareness. Encouraging women to get mammograms and do regular self-exams correctly can mean the difference in prevention and early detection that can save a life.

As with any charitable endeavor you engage in, seek press coverage and invite the media, city leaders, cancer survivors and socially influential members of your community to attend. While seeking publicity may feel self-serving because it can be beneficial to your business, it is equally as valuable in attracting attention and donations to the causes you are supporting and what is more, you are setting an example for others to follow.

So when it comes to tooting your own horn on a charitable endeavor, make as much noise as you can!

lots of locks for locks of love - www.locksoflove.org

One of my favorite cancer-related charities, Locks of Love provides wigs made of real human hair for those battling cancers and other illnesses that result in hair loss. You cannot measure the impact this makes to someone who is dealing not only with a terrible illness, but also with the ravages it imposes on the body, or even the damage caused by the treatments themselves. Providing wigs made of real human hair, donated out of love is more than cosmetic; it helps restore the emotional well being, self-esteem and dignity of someone struggling in so many areas. You can get all of the requirements including how to properly cut, store and send the hair to Locks of Love on their web site. This makes a great salon event for fund raising; donate cuts in return for monetary donations of (any) clients as well as hair that qualifies for the program.

3 day walk - susan g. komen
www.the3day.org | ww5.komen.org

The Susan G. Komen 3 Day Walk is an experience that can change your life, regardless of your connection to Breast Cancer. The ultimate team building exercise, putting a team together for the Walk made up of friends, coworkers, or clients will do more than just raise funds. You will meet women who walk in honor of lost loved ones, loved ones in a current battle, and you will meet courageous women battling breast cancer and cancer survivors.

Hundreds of women and men come together each year in cities throughout the U.S. to raise money for Susan G. Komen for the Cure and the National Philanthropic Trust Breast Cancer Fund. They take their commitment to end breast cancer to the limit, walking 60 miles over the course of three days. Eighty-five percent of the net proceeds of this event go to Susan G. Komen for the Cure. According to their web site, every advancement in breast cancer research, treatment, education and prevention in the last 25 years has been touched by a 'Komen for the Cure' Grant. The remaining fifteen percent of net funds goes to the National Philanthropic Trust Breast Cancer Fund to provide a permanent endowment for ongoing support of breast cancer initiatives.

fund raising

Highly organized charities can provide you with support and a myriad of ideas for fund raising. Check with your tax professional to ensure that you structure your fund raising efforts appropriately to ensure that donors contributions are tax deductible. Work within the guidelines and rules of the charities.

color a world without cancer

Hold an in-salon contest and invite clients, their children, children of employees, or even invite a local elementary school to participate in a coloring or art contest titled, "Color a World Without Cancer." The winner/s will be chosen from entries to receive a free cut and color in November. All entrants should receive a special cut and color offer from you. Write a press release and send copies of finalists work to your local newspaper for added awareness.

donated services

Donate your services in-salon or in-hospital for patients or their families and caregivers. Invite clients to donate or underwrite salon services or products.

all in a day's work

Ask clients for donations in lieu of payment for services on a given, publicized day. Ask staff to participate if they can. While charitable giving guidelines prohibit you from dictating a specified donation amount, you can recommend a suggested donation amount. In the spirit of generosity, most participants will meet or even exceed your suggested donation. Ask clients to participate in matching donations. Invite a member of the charity, local men and women affected by cancer, civic leaders and the media to the salon for a reception to present your donation.

all popped up

October is National Popcorn Poppin' Month, so give each client a bag of freshly popped popcorn, a bag of kettle corn or a sampling of your favorite popcorn flavor. Partner with an equipment rental company and promote their business while renting a machine for the month (at a free or discounted rate). Or sell popcorn or bags of microwave popcorn with proceeds going to your favorite cancer charity. Work with local merchants to stage a cross-marketed sidewalk popcorn sale or special charity fund raiser event.

don't get spooked

If local merchants sponsor a Halloween event, get involved. Give out candy all month long to clients along with an invitation to your Halloween event. If you are not hosting trick or treating for kids, throw a Halloween mixer for grown ups instead in partnership with a local restaurant, caterer or other business.

a year to heal

Work with local support services or solicit nominations from clients to 'adopt' a local cancer patient or their family members and donate a year of free haircut services or solicit donations of money or needed goods (food, donations toward uncovered health care services, salon services and products, clothing, furniture, supplies, etc.) from clients. Provide regular updates to your clients about how their donations are making a difference. Check with the recipient of your attentions beforehand and share only the information they feel comfortable sharing. You can tell clients about the general conditions a person is facing and provide updates without revealing their identity.

treat-or-treat

No client should leave your salon this month without a little something sweet for themselves. Cross-market and partner with a local chocolatier to provide branded chocolates or candies at a discounted rate in exchange for promoting their services to your clients. These would also be great to stock for retail sale or give-away with gift certificate purchase for client holiday gifts, or for your next Valentine's and Mother's Day promotions.

be corny

If local fresh produce sellers put on a Corn Maze, see if you can rent booth space or provide coupons with treats such as small salon-branded goody bags of candy corn or popcorn that can be given to patrons who come to tackle the Corn Maze or other activities. Include items and special offers for the staff and owner as well.

october is dental hygiene month

If you partnered with a Dentist in August, continue cross-marketing efforts by promoting their hygiene services to your clients in return for a referral fee or cross-marketing. Create a hair care or hair color care 'hygiene' offer for their clients and speak to the needs of particular hair types when it comes to cleansing.

Some dentists and orthodontists host a Halloween candy exchange where children can trade in tooth-decaying sweets for gift cards or other items. Consider participating in their candy exchange by giving their patients a coupon for a free haircut, retail product, gift-with-service or free add-on service, or host a candy exchange of your own.

october is long range planning month

Set aside time this month to brainstorm with staff or other professionals and set goals for the coming year for your salon or spa in service and retail sales, professional development and education. Consult with your distributor sales consultant or a professional business or marketing consultant for additional expertise or to begin lining up classes for staff and the support you need for sales initiatives.

October Observances and Charitable Causes

October is Breast Cancer Awareness Month. Just as important as finding the cure is prevention and early detection. Contact your local health care or cancer treatment center, or go online to get information that you can provide in-salon via posters, station talkers, or hand out with receipts to raise awareness, promote healthy living and proper self-exams. Write press releases to increase community awareness.

In addition to Locks of Love (www.locksoflove.org) and the Susan G. Komen 3-Day Walk (www.the3day.org) you can support the City of Hope (www.cityofhope.org) or get personally involved by supporting your local cancer treatment center or children's hospital.

I was widowed at the age of 22. My first husband was treated at Cancer Treatment Centers of America for (incurable) metastasized melanoma. If you have seen their ads on TV, you know that Cancer Treatment Centers of America provide treatment to patients that some cancer centers view as 'incurable' (www.cancercenter.com).

I can speak to the truth in their commercials; Cancer Treatment Centers of America treat patients holistically and allow patients to customize their treatment in a way that many traditional centers do not. CTC and many other cancer treatment facilities also provide free or low cost housing for family members and would welcome your donated funds, services, or products.

October Planning and Tasks

Select from manufacturers retail promotions for those which will support your November, December and Holiday planned marketing and promotions. Design and print (or order) marketing and support materials needed for coming events and promotions.

Purchase any last items and firm up partnerships needed for your November 'holiday fair' event or sale. Capturing holiday sales ahead of the big retail push that traditionally begins at Thanksgiving is imperative to healthy holiday season sales; discretionary dollars designated by your customers for gift giving will disappear quickly once Thanksgiving hits.

Planning for Holiday and November-December should be nearly complete, and you should be publicizing and gearing up for your Holiday Shop retail event in November. Make sure all partners are on board and that their employees have scripts for making gift certificate and retail gift suggestions to clients. Consider an internal incentive or contest to ensure that your marketing partners and their employees focus on supporting your shared sales goals and event initiatives.

Communicate in October

Items to include in your e-mail or print newsletter, e-mail, web site and direct mail communications this month:

- » October, November, December and Holiday events and promotions
- » Strong messaging to promote sales of gift certificates and products you offer that would make ideal holiday and hostess gifts
- » Promotions expiring in October, new products coming for the holiday season
- » 'Save the date' announcements for holiday events
- » Announce September contest winners and October contest opportunities
- » Last minute openings on the books

October Calendar / Suggested Communications and Tasks Schedule

SUN	MON	TUE	WED	THU	FRI	SAT
1st week of Month						
1st of October - Merchandise for October 1st of October – Begin collecting entries for October contests						
		Order signage, event supplies and promotional materials for November-December promotions			Send October Newsletter with coupons, announce contests and winners, new products and services coming events, openings still on the books, events and promotions	
2nd week of Month						
Set aside time for long range planning; create marketing blueprint for next year		Order in gifts, salon-branded items, impulse buy and other items for November-December			Write press releases for any events/results reporting or future events / charitable focus	
3rd week of Month						
Begin marketing for holiday		Finalize planning for November-December promotions			Send October "last chance" promotions and openings on the books e-mail and/or direct mail	
4th week of Month						
Last day of October – Take down any October-only promotions Last day of October – Draw October contest winners						
		Order event supplies, postcards, gifts and salon-branded items needed for November-December promotions			Send November focus e-mail / direct mail with strong holiday gift suggestion and messaging	

October Worksheets

$_____ Retail Sales Goal

Promotions_____

_____

_____

_____

_____

$_____ Avg. Retail/Client

$_____ Retail Sales Results

$_____ Service Sales Goal

Promotions_____

_____

_____

_____

_____

$_____ Avg. Service/Client

$_____ Service Sales Results

$_____ Event Revenues Goal

Events _____

_____

_____

_____

_____

#_____ Attending Event/s

#_____ Apts/Booked at Event

$_____ Event/s Sales

$_____ Total Event/s Results

$_____ Charity/Fund Raising Goal

Charity Events _____

_____

_____

_____

_____

#_____ Attending Event/s

#_____ Apts/Booked at Event

$_____ Charity Event/s Sales

$_____ Total Charity Results

October Marketing Summary

Marketing Partners: _____

_____

_____

_____

Marketing Collateral Needed (or Used): _____

_____

_____

Other Efforts:

#_____ Number of Clients New to Salon

%_____ Client Retention Rate (90 days)

Retention Efforts: _____

_____

or % _____ Clients Rebooked at Appointment

$_____ Gift Certificate Sales

#_____ Contacts added to marketing / e-mail database

November

remodel marketing

Physically renovating your space – even just repainting – can be expensive. But remodeling your marketing program to support next year's goals for retail sales, service promotions, event, client attraction and retention can be done at little cost and return big revenues.

Think about your marketing strategies in the same way that you would rearrange, remodel and renovate your salon and spa interior to meet stylist and client needs, prepare to launch new services, and make room for retail changes. Tailor your marketing strategies to suit your strengths and your interests and the things that you most love to do, just as you would remodel and redecorate your salon from the standpoint of your own perspective and preferences.

Many people think of external activities when it comes to marketing, such as advertising, promotions, postcards, e-mails, flyers, and coupons, etc. But remodeling is first and foremost a reflection of what is inside, and you should always look inward first when it comes to marketing, because marketing begins – and ends – with the reflection of your brand.

No advertising, promotional, incentive, rewards or other initiative can go beyond the strength of your brand in the long run. Before you start knocking down marketing "walls" or putting in new marketing "fixtures," take a good hard look at your current brand features.

Examine what you "see" when you take an honest look at what makes your brand strong (or weak) but also examine what your clients "see" when they look at your salon.

> » What do you love the most about your job or your salon?
>
> » What are your strengths?
>
> » What do your clients love most about you?
>
> » What do they take time to compliment?
>
> » Which services and products have the strongest followings and which have the most heartwarming stories?
>
> » Which of your staff members have cultivated the most loyal clients, and why?

Before you remodel your marketing for the coming year, identify those characteristics you do not want to lose. Identify the strengths

> employ *your* strengths and interests

that you want to accentuate and the details about your business that you most desire to stand out, and then gear your remodeling plan to make the most of those things while also reflecting new initiatives.

As you launch into remodeling your marketing for the coming year, you should have an "artist's sketch" in mind of what your business should look like after the remodel is complete. Just as you would not remodel or redecorate your salon without a vision and plan for the end result, you need to know what your end result should look like for marketing as well.

If your top priority for the New Year is new client attraction, then your remodeling plan should be highly focused on events and outreach activities designed to draw new clients in. If your goal is to increase retail sales, then your marketing plan should reflect aggressive strategies for educating and promoting retail products. If you have a revolving door and want to increase client retention, then your marketing efforts need to be focused on what needs to change *after* the client walks in the door, rather than simply attracting more clients.

No matter what your top priorities are for the coming year and how obvious you think your corporate goals are, you cannot assume that all of your employees will be on board. Your marketing remodeling plan needs to provide clear training, motivational, incentive and accountability plans for all employees.

As you construct your remodeled marketing plan, remember to be aware of external factors and constraints.

> » What are local conditions like, and what are local conditions like for your major client demographic groups?

> » Where is business growing?

> » Who are the major employers you could reach out to with group promotions?

> » Are there businesses new to your community that would want to pool resources and ideas with you to create client-attraction events?

> » Is now the time for you to take a leadership role in developing a "buy local" initiative in your community?

| use what's hot now |

Finally, you would not renovate your salon and put 20 year old equipment, fixtures and tools in it and you certainly wouldn't use 20 year old irons and dryers on clients and expect great results. The point being that you need to employ the newest technology such as the internet, e-mail, social media sites, text reminders, etc., in your marketing plan to reach your goals, again, most of which can be done at little to no cost beyond your time. The internet can offer you much more than just a web site and the ability to send e-mails to clients. The web is now filled with niche communities and tools where you can build community online, such as Facebook, MySpace or Twitter. You can create a following, keep customers apprised of salon news, staff and client spotlight news, promote charitable causes, events in the salon, offer coupons and time-limited offers and so much more.

A computer, an internet connection, and a few minutes a day is all it takes to keep in touch with your customers and your community online; compare that with older and more costly practices like phoning or mailing invitations!

Approach next year's marketing plan with the same techniques that you would a remodel, renovation or redecoration – focused on building out your business beautifully in the coming year!

November Event
and Promotion Ideas

For some salons and spas, holiday retail sales can represent 25% or more of total retail or gift certificate sales for the year. To focus on anything but holiday sales and events in November or December is to lose ground not only in the current year but in the year to come.

It's not just about retail sales, gift certificates sold for holiday gift giving are not only a source of revenue, they are also a means of acquiring new clients and building client loyalty. At no time in recent history have customers been so focused on value and savings. Your holiday gift and retail strategy must focus on what your clients want and need.

'tis the season for
holiday bundles and goodies

Holiday sales do not happen by accident, and only a small percentage will occur in-salon by impulse or as a last-minute choice by stymied gift givers. To have a successful holiday season and capture what might represent the lion's share of your salon's annual retail or gift certificate sales business, you have to plan ahead, beginning as early as August. Build and implement a strategy designed to meet your client's needs, sell through retail and gift certificates, and gain business and new clients for the new year.

To make holiday sales, you have to get people in the door to buy them, and you might only see your clients once or twice during the busy holiday season. So how do you capture a bigger piece of the holiday gift market?

Key to maximizing holiday and gift certificate sales will be events, partnerships and cross-marketing efforts. If you have been building partnerships with fitness instructors, cosmetic dental or medical professionals, gift boutiques, wine shops, costume jewelry sales, or other independent sales professionals, now is the time to conduct a strong cross-marketing promotion for the holidays. Enlist their help for commissions or work in trade to sell gift certificates or even retail products on your behalf and to create cross-promotions, bundling their services or goods with yours.

In September and October, purchase salon-branded holiday chocolates, wine, tanks, t-shirts, lip gloss, brushes or combs, nail files and other impulse buy type gift items to boost retail sales throughout the holiday season. These items also make great client gifts and extend the brand of your salon or spa beyond your walls.

Help clients get a jump start on New Year's Resolutions with gift certificate packages that include martial arts, fitness, jazzercise, yoga or dietary instruction to get the body in shape along with cut and color "exercises" designed to get the hair in shape in 3, 6 or even 12 month "membership" packages.

holiday shop

In early to mid-November, have some fun and jump start holiday sales by holding a Holiday Shop in-salon or cooperatively in a business partner's space. Clients will focus mainly on shopping at malls and department stores beginning around Thanksgiving; getting ahead of the holiday can make a big difference.

If you cannot hold a Holiday Shop event in your salon or with a partnering business, contact local churches and schools to find out about participating in their holiday bazaars. If you participate in an off-site event, be sure that your kiosk includes more than just gifts and gift certificate sales. Have copies of your business cards, menus, contest entry forms for data collection and ads for coming events and promotions displayed for clients to take or used as bag stuffers. Bring a travel kit and do free mini makeovers, mini manicures, quick style fixes, sample skin and hair care products, etc. If you are a stylist, schedule a succession of 2-3 models to come so that you can show attendees your style and demonstrate use and benefits of products that they can purchase from your kiosk.

Feature a new-client incentive in your materials to entice shoppers to give you a try before the end of December. Make sure all take-away materials have your contact information. Your in-salon Holiday Shop should be well-merchandised, from the outside in. Entice shoppers in from the outside through the use of store front areas and displays visible from the doorway. Make your event larger by partnering and cross-marketing with local businesses to reach out to multiple client bases in promoting holiday specials for all businesses represented.

Purchase non-traditional items that clients would be likely to purchase on their own or in conjunction with gift certificates (such as branded "bling" T-shirts and tanks, chocolates, candies, wine, candles, interior decor items, holiday dishes, gloves, hats, notebooks, pens, jewelry, lip glosses, skin lotions, etc.,) as well as traditional salon-type gift offerings like plush robes or terry hoodies, nail files, brushes, combs, hair accessories or hair or skin care travel products.

The possibilities are endless!

holiday parties

Just as you catered to prom goers, brides and graduates in the summer, you can cater to holiday party goers now. Partner with a local limo service, restaurants, and party destinations to create a package including a makeover or spa package prior to the event with a champagne or non-alcoholic sparkling cocktail to get things started.

get inspired

November is Inspirational Role Model Month. Take nominations and select a winner at the end of November to receive a free service in December along with the individual who nominated them. Make sure all entrants and all those making nominations receive a special promotional offer and create recognition flyers or even a press release to honor some of the most special stories.

awards show

Take your "Get Inspired" promotion one step further by partnering with other businesses to create a truly large prize package – who knows, maybe including a vacation, car, retail shopping spree – if you don't ask, you'll never know! Top off your November contest with an Awards Show, complete with pre-show makeovers for finalists, red carpet and a great meal or reception at a local restaurant, partnering with a limo service, restaurant or banquet facility and caterer, musician or band, wine shop, florist, etc. Invite local media and local civic leaders, politicians, celebrities, and socialites. Hold a silent auction for charity or holiday sale in conjunction and award winners in multiple categories, inspiring your audience with the stories of these inspirational role models. Make it an annual event!

beat the holiday blues

Many members of your community do not have holiday parties or family events to attend. Consider providing volunteer services at your local senior center and make opportunities for service or donations available to clients.

corporate holiday events and gifts

Create a pre-party reception for local businesses who are having holiday parties including party hair and makeup styling, mini-makeovers or mini-massages and a champagne toast. Or take your show on the road to corporate meetings, retreats or conventions to provide mini-services, sell retail and book appointments during corporate meeting lunch or break times. Have a plan to extend bounce back offers, and take bookings for regular appointments and provide copies of your business card and new client offers. (Attending corporate meetings is a service that you can add to your service menu and provide all year.)

stylist holiday mixer

In the hustle and bustle that comes from prepping clients for everyone else's holiday parties, don't forget your own friends and co-workers. Get out of the salon and into a holiday venue that is friendly for mixing and bringing significant others (or even families) and create a holiday event that includes your own "Inspirational Awards" for the people who mean the most to you and your business.

November Observances and Charitable Causes

The holidays are filled with sweets, but not everyone gets to enjoy them! November is National Diabetes Month and a perfect time to promote awareness and the warning signs of diabetes or pre-diabetic conditions. Partner with a local nutritionist and fitness instructor to provide literature and create cross-marketed, bundled promotions for their clients as well as yours.

November is Military Appreciation Month. What a great time to say "thank you" to the men and women who put their lives on hold and on the line for our country and freedoms, and to honor the families that sacrifice as well. Consider an event or donations to support local military men and women and their families. Take nominations from clients or contact your local base to find out about 'adopting' a military family or military family service provider and providing needed food or gifts for them for the holidays through the end of the year.

November Planning and Tasks

Purchase any last retail products needed for Holiday or November-December events and promotions. Even though these months will be hectic, set aside some time and begin to plan for January and February based on the long range plan you developed for the New Year in October. (If October came and went without development of a long range plan, set aside time for it before the end of the year.) Design and print (or order) marketing or support materials needed for coming promotions through the holidays and into next year.

Communicate in November

Items to include in your print or e-mail newsletter, e-mail, web site and direct mail communications this month:

» November, December and Holiday events and promotions

» Last minute openings, plus any extended hours for the holiday season

» Suggestions and 'how to's' for holiday makeovers or event hair or skin including hair, makeup, and skin care

» Tips for making a holiday look last all through an event from setting makeup or hair to staying hydrated, getting enough rest, and pampering services needed before and after the event

» Gift bundles, partnered promotions, suggestions and Certificates

» Promotions expiring in November, new products coming in December

November Calendar / Suggested Communications and Tasks Schedule

SUN	MON	TUE	WED	THU	FRI	SAT
1st week of Month 1st of November - Merchandise for November 1st of November – Begin collecting entries for November contests						
		Order from manufacturers retail promotions for products to support December-January-February marketing plans; design related signage			Send November Newsletter with coupons, announce contests and winners, new products and services coming events, openings still on the books, events and promotions	
2nd week of Month						
		Order event supplies, postcards, collateral, gifts and salon-branded items for December contests			Write press releases for any events/results reporting or future events / charitable focus	
3rd week of Month						
		Layout plans for January promotions			Send November "last chance" promotions and openings on the books e-mail and/or direct mail	
4th week of Month Last day of November – Take down any November-only promotions Last day of November – Draw November contest winners						
		Order event supplies, postcards, gifts and salon-branded items needed for January promotions			Send December focus e-mail / direct mail with strong holiday gift messaging	

November Worksheets

$_____ Retail Sales Goal

Promotions_____

_____

_____

_____

_____

$_____ Avg. Retail/Client

$_____ Retail Sales Results

$_____ Service Sales Goal

Promotions_____

_____

_____

_____

_____

$_____ Avg. Service/Client

$_____ Service Sales Results

$_____ Event Revenues Goal

Events _____

_____

_____

_____

_____

#_____ Attending Event/s

#_____ Apts/Booked at Event

$_____ Event/s Sales

$_____ Total Event/s Results

$_____ Charity/Fund Raising
Goal

Charity Events _____

_____

_____

_____

_____

#_____ Attending Event/s

#_____ Apts/Booked at Event

$_____ Charity Event/s Sales

$_____ Total Charity Results

November Marketing Summary

Marketing Partners: _____

_____

_____

_____

Marketing Collateral Needed (or Used): _____

_____

_____

Other Efforts:

#_____ Number of Clients New to Salon

%_____ Client Retention Rate (90 days)

Retention Efforts: _____

_____

or % _____ Clients Rebooked at Appointment

$_____ Gift Certificate Sales

#_____ Contacts added to marketing / e-mail database

December

out with the old, in with the new scene stealers

This year will be over and before you know it, you will find yourself setting out on a new year. Take some time in December to evaluate the past year and make professional as well as personal New Year's Resolutions for the coming year. You may be planning to open your own salon, expand, become an educator or platform artist, enter a competition, publish your work, select new products, or you might simply need to update your pricing and services.

No matter what your goals, putting them on paper and noting the steps required to reach them will help you to avoid procrastinating and take the first step. Sharing your goals and your time line with a trusted friend or mentor can also help you to feel more accountable toward them.

Plan now to help clients ring in the New Year (or say goodbye to the old one) with a special VIP customer reception held in-salon or at a local restaurant, wine, book or gift shop that is willing to partner with you for a cross-marketed event. Ideally, this reception will be exclusively for clients who are the most loyal and responsive to your events and promotions, rather than open to all. This VIP event should be for your most loyal clients, and especially those who are influential within their communities or within civic, political, corporate, or other mid to large-sized groups. Your goal is to create a loyal, locked in client base for the new year who will be likely to build buzz, refer friends, family and coworkers, and stay dialed-in next year.

At the reception, offer VIP-client-exclusive packages for 3, 6 or even 12 months, or offer packages that support cross-business promotions with the marketing partners you established this year. Create packages with compelling savings or add-ons; if working with other vendors, these packages should be cross-marketed to their clients as well as yours.

If you have created several strong business partnerships, hold the event in a venue large enough to accommodate a large number of clients and activities. Treat invited guests like the celebrities they are; provide them with a goody bag to take home full of freebies and offers and provide a thank you gift to all clients who enroll in a membership or purchase a package.

Provide incentives for clients to bring a new guest with them to the event, or who refer new clients to your salon in January. And remember, you don't have to give away your services or retail products; salon-branded t-shirts, tanks, and other gifts make very reasonably priced but effective "thank you" gifts for your clients and extend your brand beyond the walls of the salon.

In December you will wrap up holiday sales and clean up on holiday party makeovers. Show your appreciation to clients with special thank yous, holiday messages and gifts.

reward clients and renew rewards

Prepare for the New Year, including putting the finishing touches on your marketing plan. During the last week of December when you may be closed for the holidays or things are on the slow side, set aside time to take stock of where you are, how far you have come during the last year, and make New Year's (business) Resolutions. Set aside time to appreciate your mentors, co-workers and friends and celebrate the end of a great year – and the beginning of a promising new one!

As you plan for the New Year, take a step back to examine the experience provided to clients in your salon or spa. When *was* the last time that you truly viewed the experience from your client's point of view? It is not always easy to see things from their perspective. When you are there performing your role day in and day out, it can be easy to overlook details that might be escaping your notice simply because you have become accustomed to seeing them. One way to overcome this tendency is to actually analyze the client experience in a systematic way, from a non-traditional point of view.

Just as in theatre, the client experience occurs on a set. This set is comprised of the outside and inside of the salon, and scenes occur not only on set, but on the phone, on your website, by email, and any other touch point that your client has with you, or with any member of your salon, as well as within the salon or spa itself. The first step in improving the client experience, then, is to set the stage. As this year winds down, take your analysis of the client experience and create a new set for your salon for the new year.

Think of your salon or spa as a theater, with employees as main cast members and your clients as recurring characters. If you begin to view each client experience as a "scene" in your overall business script, you can pull apart different components in order to more properly set the stage for success.

For instance:

> When a client arrives, what do they first see, even *before* they walk into your salon? What is the first thing they see when they enter?

> Does a member of your "cast" greet each client? Are your guests provided with a comfortable waiting area? Do they know how long they will wait? Are they offered a beverage or snack? Do they know where to hang their coat? Are they shown where rest rooms are for their comfort?

> Once in the chair, how do you manage the "scene?" Are you prepared with a "script" for an effective, interactive consultation? Do you have your "timing" down? Can you speak to clients about the products you are using, and which products would enhance their home hair, skin and nail care regimens?

> How do your "regular cast members" interact with one another in front of clients?

> Have you set up "props" (retail products and displays) in order to help promote retail sales? Do you have adequate lighting and signage so clients can choose the products that would be most appropriate for their hair care needs?

> When the client leaves, how do you end the "scene?" Do you make it easy for clients to become "recurring characters" by re-booking or offering them an incentive to purchase a series of services?

> Do you regularly thank your "guest stars" – your most important clients – for their business?

> Can clients not wait to get there, or are they in a hurry to leave?

Small indulgences, small moments of escape, small pleasures. When the stage is set it is easy to move toward incorporating small moments of indulgence to enhance the client experience. Look for ways that you can treat clients to moments of luxury, relaxation, aromatherapy and other sensory indulgences to enhance their experience, set your business apart from others, and keep them coming back for more. A dark chocolate you ask them to sample in the chair or at the point of purchase. A demonstration of how to use a room spray and blow dryer to diffuse fragrance at home. The gift of a genuine compliment and a genuine thank you to every client.

who is speaking for the client?

Draw other actors to your stage. Make a list of businesses in your physical proximity or who are connected to you through family, friends, or clients. Set out to contact each of these businesses to create cooperative and cross marketing opportunities to support your marketing goals during the coming year. For instance, if you want to hold a fashion show, partner with a boutique clothier, shoe store, caterer, wine shop, and an esthetician and show not only the latest fashions and accessories, but also demonstrate how to combine essential wardrobe elements creatively, how to create a seasonal hair and makeup look – all in a setting where clients can also bring friends to enjoy the event as well as some great refreshments. Invite your catering partner to share party planning tips or recipes (or use your fashion show event as a springboard for the next event – a Party Planning Workshop!) One good idea can be the seed to launch a series of events, drawing your clients into closer relationship with your business and resulting in new clients.

As you plan to write your marketing "script" for next year, create events and promotions for each month purposefully designed to create moments of (client) self-centered indulgence: wine and chocolate; a fashion show; mini-massages; a bridal fair; a demo on applying eye-shadow before they leave the salon; a workshop on personal development or empowerment; a charitable campaign, food or clothing drive to bring some of the simple pleasures of life to those less fortunate in your community – the possibilities are endless. View the value of promotions and services from the client's point of view – not the manufacturer's, distributor's, or even your own – and create messages that highlight the client-pleasure factor.

December Event
and Promotion Ideas

wrapping up the holiday season
out with the old, in with the new (year)

December should be a strong month for gift certificate sales, particularly if you remind clients in the chair and in your communications about what great gifts they make as well as highlighting compelling packages you created for the New Year.

This is a great time to renew the men's or women's hair cut packages you sold earlier in the year or to create a new rebooking or client loyalty programs such as (for women) saving $6 when they rebook within 6 weeks of an appointment, or (for men) saving $3 when they rebook within 3 weeks, or any other package of services which must be used within 3 or 6 month time period.

Rebooking and package incentives can also be a great way to soften a price increase for your most loyal customers. If you consider the alternative, that without a strong rebooking program your female clients in a down economy might wait 8-10 weeks to rebook, you will make more money with your existing clients even with a $6 discount. Pre-selling packages at a discount that mandate a specified rebooking time line is more profitable than if clients extend the time between appointments by even an extra week.

Take stock of the last year, analyzing initiatives, marketing efforts, events, and cross-marketing partnerships against your goals. Take note of any unexpected benefits from the programs you ran, what worked well, what you enjoyed the most, problems you did not anticipate, or where you fell short in efforts to market, promote or create buzz around your promotions.

Consider speaking to a few key customers about what type of programs or packages would induce them to take action. Asking a few trusted clients to participate in a focus group and garnering customer feedback on a regular basis can help you to construct more effective promotions and events, avoid unforeseen pitfalls and give clients what they really want from you as you continue creating a larger role for your business in their lives. Make adjustments to your annual marketing plan to prepare it for launch.

client gifts for all price ranges

Remembering that you may only see clients once in November and December, order client gifts before November to ensure that you have an opportunity to thank your most important clients, co-workers and friends. Holiday client gifts and add-on incentives provide you with the opportunity to partner with a local chocolatier, candy maker, coffee shop, wine shop or boutique and to order branded client gifts for retail sales, creating cross-marketed opportunities for both businesses.

Inexpensive client gifts and free-with-purchase incentives such as nail files, brushes, lip glosses, and other stocking stuffers, purse or travel items generally will not break the bank and will continue to extend your brand beyond the walls of the salon as well as making recipients feel like valued members of your inner circle.

Consider offering a buy-one, get-one gift certificate promotion where the buyer receives a $20 certificate for themselves with purchase of $100 (or more) in gift certificates for others.

If your client gift budget is $0, you can still give a meaningful gift to everyone on your list, including clients and staff. In 2009, inspired by a popular religious book and group study, the owner of the salon I patronize (Dawn Taylor, Salon Bella Dea in Auburn, Washington) wrote a personal letter to her clients telling them how they have impacted her life over the years. She thanked them not only for their business, but also thanked those clients who knew her parents and had prayed for her mom while she was battling cancer, for all that she feels that she learns from her clients, and how much she appreciates them entrusting her with their hair.

She said that the idea behind her letter was to tell people what she would want to tell them if she knew she had only a short time left to do so. Without being morbid, the result was a letter written to people telling them they have impacted her life in ways they might not even know, inspiring them to continue to make a personal difference in lives where they can, never knowing how much even a small act of kindness can mean. The gift she gave to her clients was nearly free, but priceless!

save $6 in 6 presold

For loyal customers, savings on services that ensure they will be back into the salon more often is a win-win, where you get both wins! For women, pre-sell a package of 6 haircuts at your current year's rates plus a $6 per haircut savings, with an expiration date exactly 36 weeks from the date of issuance. You will ensure repeat visits every 6 weeks (chances are getting your female client in-salon more often than usual) and you will make more money than if they extended their time between services by even one week.

Since the services are presold, you will also have use of the money in advance with the opportunity to gain interest or invest in such a way that you make the money work for you. For men, pre-sell a package of 6 haircuts at your current year's rates plus a savings of $3 each, with an expiration date exactly 18 weeks from issuance.

retro rewards

Say thank you to your most valuable clients in some special way and extend your brand by gifting branded travel mugs, t-shirts or tanks, unique nail files or other creative, buzz-worthy, low-cost items. Sell some, too!

toys for tots

Support the Marines annual 'Toys for Tots' campaign or choose your own charity; contact your local social support services office or a church for a family to 'adopt,' or set up a "gift tree" where your clients can choose gifts to purchase for local needy families or donate money.

and bingo was his name-o

December is National Bingo Month. Create a special 'Bingo' contest in conjunction with partnering local businesses where clients receive a free gift or entry in a drawing for free service (and/or prizes from other businesses) in January if they visit each of the businesses on a card or flyer. Credit for this idea belongs to my friend Celia Bender, marketing diva and owner of Chameleon Productions, who employed this contest as part of a regional "buy local" campaign effort. Make sure that all entries, from all businesses, make it to your print and e-mail marketing contact database and receive special offers for the New Year.

Many Bingo-loving seniors may feel left out during this time of year. Partner with a local senior center to host a holiday Bingo Tournament, enlisting business partners to create special prizes designed to bring seniors into the salon and into your partners' businesses.

party on

Partner with local limo, shuttle, hotel, or related services to offer clients special packages including mini-makeovers or blow out and styling plus transportation to or from their big holiday or New Year's party.

Host or provide mini spa or makeover services for corporate holiday parties where you will also have the opportunity to sell retail products, collect contact information, and follow up with a special offer for January.

December Observances and Charitable Causes

You will not have to look far to find a family – or even a client – in need in your community. Local support services organizations, missions, or homeless shelters can provide you with information about those in need in your community and how your clients can best support relief and rehabilitation efforts.

Make your December charitable focus a local one. Raise donated gifts or monies for a local family or support services organization, such as your local mission or homeless shelter. Go the extra mile and volunteer on your own, or as a group of staff, to help serve meals or even provide services to needy families or at your local shelter. Publicize your efforts in order to bring more support to the organization.

December Planning and Tasks

Choose from manufacturers retail promotions to support the promotions and events you have planned for January and February including New Year packages and Resolution-Helper partnerships with fitness instructors or facilities, martial arts studios, jazzercise or dance studios and others.

Put final adjustments into your marketing and business plan for the first half of next year and ensure that your business partners are lined up to support efforts to wrap up the old year and begin the new one. Create a loyalty or rewards program for the New Year.

Plan a New Year's party for your business partners, co-workers and friends to say thank you and get the New Year off to a good start. Or, plan a reception or pre-New Year's Eve party makeover package for clients. Purchase salon-branded items to help kick start efforts and events in the New Year.

Sketch out a plan for February events including a Valentine's Day gift and gift certificate push.

Communicate in December

Items to include in your print or e-mail newsletter, e-mail, web site and direct mail communications this month:

- » Any promotions expiring in December
- » Packages available for purchase for the New Year to avoid any planned service or manufacturer's products price increases
- » Last minute gift and holiday ideas
- » Holiday party ideas, makeover ideas and tips and products for clients to help ensure that their party look lasts until well after midnight
- » Suggest that clients purchase spa services for gifts as well as for themselves during the hectic holiday season or as a reward for making it into a new year
- » January and February 'save the date' for events through Valentine's Day
- » Last minute openings on the books and best time to book for holiday party preparation

December Calendar / Suggested Communications and Tasks Schedule

SUN	MON	TUE	WED	THU	FRI	SAT
1st week of Month						
1st of December - Merchandise for December 1st of December – Begin collecting entries for December contests						
		Order signage, event supplies and promotional materials for January promotions			Send December Newsletter with coupons, announce contests and winners, new products and services coming events, openings still on the books, events and promotions	
2nd week of Month						
		Order in gifts, salon-branded items, impulse buy and other items for January-February			Write press releases for any events/results reporting or future events / charitable focus	
3rd week of Month						
Begin marketing for New Year		Layout plans for January-February promotions			Send December "last chance" promotions and openings on the books e-mail and/or direct mail	
4th week of Month						
Last day of December – Take down any December-only promotions Last day of December – Draw December contest winners						
		Order event supplies, postcards, gifts and salon- January-February promotions			Send January focus e-mail / direct mail	

December Worksheets

$_____ Retail Sales Goal

Promotions_____

_____

_____

_____

_____

$_____ Avg. Retail/Client

$_____ Retail Sales Results

$_____ Service Sales Goal

Promotions_____

_____

_____

_____

_____

$_____ Avg. Service/Client

$_____ Service Sales Results

$_____ Event Revenues Goal

Events _____

_____

_____

_____

_____

#_____ Attending Event/s

#_____ Apts/Booked at Event

$_____ Event/s Sales

$_____ Total Event/s Results

$_____ Charity/Fund Raising
Goal

Charity Events _____

_____

_____

_____

_____

#_____ Attending Event/s

#_____ Apts/Booked at Event

$_____ Charity Event/s Sales

$_____ Total Charity Results

December Marketing Summary

Marketing Partners: _____

_____

_____

_____

Marketing Collateral Needed (or Used): _____

_____

_____

Other Efforts:

#_____ Number of Clients New to Salon

%_____ Client Retention Rate (90 days)

Retention Efforts: _____

_____

or % _____ Clients Rebooked at Appointment

$_____ Gift Certificate Sales

#_____ Contacts added to marketing / e-mail database

acknowledgements and resources

12 Months of Marketing for Salon and Spa
special thanks to

Sydney Berry and George Learned, Owners, Salon Services & Supplies, Renton, WA
www.salonservicesnw.com
For modeling their passion for the professional beauty industry with unparalleled industry and love, and loving their customers with unparalleled passion. Thank you for teaching me so much and unleashing me to do the things that I do best.

Jessee Skittrall, Salon Owner, National Colorist and Educator (aka: kadus guy)
www.youtube.com/user/KadusGuy | www.absoluthair.com
Because you are who you are, because you exemplify the creative, joyful, artistic and sacrificial spirit of the industry, and for picking me up that day someone demolished me. You approach life with a spirit of unlimited possibilities that is contagious!

Dawn Taylor, Owner, Salon Bella Dea, Auburn, WA
www.salonbelladea.com
For loving your community and your customers enough to show up, day in and day out, and love us where we are. For your prayers and encouragement. For looking out for me when I didn't know anyone was watching. For the best hair cuts I have ever had, and a brow wax that you just can't put a price on.

John Schmidt, East Coast Salon Services, Runnemede, NJ
www.eastcoastsalon.com
Because you keep working and never give up, and because you meet even my zaniest ideas with enthusiasm. Thank you for your continued friendship and support. "You know what you did."

John Busch, Lithtex NW - www.lithtexnw.com
Without question, the finest printer in the business, in my opinion. Lithtex NW has saved my clients money and met deadlines that were not meet-able.   They don't tell me when a project is going to be ready. Instead, they ask, "When do you need it."   With special thanks to owner John Busch, who believes in people. Thank you for always egging me on with unbridled enthusiasm.   "EB"

January
New Year's
2nd Week of January: Women's Empowerment Week

February
American Heart Month
An Affair to Remember Month
Creative Romance Month
2nd Week of February: Dump Your Significant Jerk Week
2nd Week of February: Jell-O Week

March
Employee Spirit Month
National Nutrition Month
3rd Week in March: National Wellderly (Well-Elderly) Week
March 1: National Beer Day
March 17: St. Patrick's Day

April
International Client Loyalty Month
National Card and Letter Writing Month
Jazz Appreciation Month
Stress Awareness Month

May
Date Your Mate Month
Women's Health Care Month
May 5: Cinco de Mayo
1st Tuesday in May: National Teacher's Day
2nd Sunday in May: Mother's Day

June
Cancer from the Sun Month
3rd Sunday in June: Father's Day

July
Family Reunion Month
National Hot Dog Month
National Ice Cream Month
National Recreation and Parks Month
July 5th: National Workaholics Day

(continued)

August
Back to School and College for Students and Teachers
2nd Week of August: National Smile Week

September
Healthy Aging Month
4th Week of September: National Dog Week
September 8: International LIteracy Day
September 10: Swap Ideas Day

October
Breast Cancer Awareness Month
Dental Hygiene Month
Long Range Planning Month
Popcorn Poppin' Month
October 31: Halloween

November
Inspirational Role Models Month
Military Family Appreciation Month
National Diabetes Month

December
Bingo Month
Write a Friend Month
Christmas, New Year's

7761029R0

Made in the USA
Charleston, SC
07 April 2011